FROM GRIEF TO GLORY

by

LEE ETHEL STEEDLEY

My Story as told to

Bestselling Author Barbara H. Martin

Thank You!
To - Anthony - 12-12-19
Love & Blessing.
Lee Ethel Smith Perkins Steedley

In Memory of
My Mother

Queen Esther Smith

Foreword

This is not a book about tragedy, but a story of God's goodness in the midst of it. Neither is it about instant answers, but about grace, mercy and strength supplied by Him in times when we need them most.

Life happens and when it does, we are ill prepared to face the giants that come our way. God knows they are there and He is not surprised or shocked when they come against us, but has prepared for us a way to deal with them which does not require our own strength, but His.

Grief is a necessary time, ordained by God, to allow our soul to heal. It is not a sign of lack of faith, but rather the Lord giving us time to rest in Him.

The three biggest giants we face during times of loss are fear, hopelessness and anger. They play on our feelings of having been left alone and the certainty it will be that way for the rest of our lives. That in turn can sometimes result in a deep anger either against the one we lost for having left us, or against God for allowing it to happen.

This is when His love, grace and mercy undergirds us in a gentle, barely recognizable way. He will keep us hidden in His love until we are ready to stop struggling and crawl out from under the darkness. It is then we are able to reach for His love, power and strength to not just face another day, but find a better life. It is one He has prepared for us from the beginning if we allow Him to lead us, and so gain the faith to accept what was and walk in confidence toward what is yet to come.

If you are in the midst of dealing with the loss of a loved one, allow this story of the sudden death of my husband and two years later, that of my son, to comfort and encourage you. Let me share with you, how you too can find hope, strength and even joy if you allow God to help you and walk with you every step of the way, because of His love and His promise in Hebrews 13:5

"I will never leave you nor forsake you."

LEE ETHEL SMITH PERKINS 1992

FROM GRIEF…

PART ONE

I am a Survivor of Enormous Loss

I am a survivor of enormous loss,
and wonder, what I ever did wrong
to be in this dark place.
I hear the doctor's voice,
Your husband died,
we don't know why.
And then,
another loss, this time my son.
I want to run away.
I am a survivor of enormous loss.

They are not talking to me,
and yet, I feel the pain.
I touch my son's young, beautiful face
one last time, clinging to hope
I will see him again.
I am a survivor of enormous loss.

I worry about my future and know
I will never be a wife and mother.
How can I understand?
All I can say,
Lord Jesus, help me.
Why, why, why?
I am a survivor of enormous loss.

And yet I dream of smiling someday,
of being a light to others,
by giving them hope to live,
to love and laugh again.
I am a survivor of enormous loss.

The Perkins Family
From L or R
Micah – Lee Ethel - Allen

Chapter 1

A Day like any other Day

𝕴t was a day like any other day and yet it would change my life forever. There was no warning, no premonition, just the anticipation Allen was coming home from the hospital.

I had left church early that Sunday to make sure I was there when the doctor released him. It was merely a hernia operation and everything had gone well. I had given a praise report an hour earlier during the service, not just for the surgery, but Allen had re-dedicated his life back to the Lord last night while his parents were visiting. His mother, a strong, godly woman, had prayed with him as he gave his heart back to Jesus. On the way to the hospital I was filled with gratitude. Allen had been getting slack about his faith lately and stopped attending church regularly, because work had taken over his time.

Thank you, Lord, now we will be a family in church and at home again the way we used to be, I thought as I walked down the long hall to his room.

When I got to the door, I was wondering why it was closed, until I saw the doctor and a nurse standing by Allen's bed. He was lying there with his eyes closed, looking very serious. Before I could say anything, the doctor looked at me with a strange look and said in an even stranger tone,

"I am sorry, but we lost your husband, Mrs. Perkins."

Allen was a jokester and I knew he had put the doctor up to this. With a big smile I walked over to him and poked him on the arm and said,

"Doctor, there is no way you can lose a 6"2' guy." Turning to Allen, I laughed,

"Ok, big guy, this isn't funny, you can open your eyes now."

"You don't understand," the doctor said, more urgently this time, "your husband is dead."

The smile froze on my lips. My mind did not want to register what I had heard. Everything around me went into slow motion amidst a fog filled with only one thought. *This has to be a joke! Why isn't anyone laughing?*

"Yes, Ethel, he really died." It was Allen's brother Junior. I only now realized he was in the room. "I was with him when he died," he added quietly, trying not to cry as he went on, "We were talking and then, suddenly, he couldn't breathe. I rang for the nurse and she gave him oxygen, thinking it would help. It did for a minute, but then he got worse and she called a code blue. They forgot I was in the room and I saw the whole thing, but then toward the end they made me leave, so I did not get to be with him when he died."

"We have no idea why your husband died until we have the results of the autopsy," the doctor said. "We are puzzled, because the surgery went fine and we are at a loss at what happened. I was going to send him home today," he added with compassion. "Mrs. Perkins, I am so sorry for your loss, we did all we could. Do you need medication to help you calm down?"

I don't even know if I answered him, because I stood by Allen, staring at him in a state of shock, numb and unable to talk. I stroked his face and only one thought kept repeating in my mind like a loop. *This can't be. He was perfectly fine, ready to come home. This is just a dream and I will wake up and laugh with him like I always do when he makes his dumb jokes. Please open your eyes, Allen and tell me this is only a joke!*

With eyes filled with tears, I suddenly realized he was gone! Allen was gone! I began to cry uncontrollably and the nurse put her arm around me. In that instant I knew my life had changed forever.

It was in the evening, I sat in my favorite chair in our bedroom. Actually, now it was my bedroom. I was alone! Feelings of anger, fear and being lost enveloped me like a cloud. It felt like a dark place, scary and painful. *I don't like it here,* I thought and wanted to leave, but something held me back. It felt like there was a heavy chain across my chest and I had trouble breathing. *How did I get here? Why did you leave me Allen?* I wanted to scream, but no sound came out. I wanted to run, but my legs wouldn't move and I stared at the bed. *I will never be able to sleep in here without you there with me.* I started to cry again, wondering if there were any tears left.

My mind went back to the day we met. He was a young, brash, handsome young man, his hair cut in a full afro with a mustache to match. His brown eyes had a sparkle in them when he smiled at me. I wasn't too impressed, because I had my eyes on another guy who was cuter and really nice. But I had to admit, Allen was handsome with his 6"2' frame, a trim body from his recent military service, and looking very sure of himself with his 24 years. I could definitely tell right away he was full of himself, pushy and forward. Maybe that turned me off, I don't remember. I was at a party for the Penn Relay Race at the home of my friend Sylvia in Philadelphia. We were a bunch of college kids having fun. Allen was invited because he was a friend of Sylvia's brother. During the evening he kept hanging around me, not giving up in spite of my somewhat stand-offish behavior, until finally, he worked up the courage to ask me out.

"I don't know," I answered with disinterest in my voice. "I live in New York and I'm sure you wouldn't want to come all the way there to date me." At twenty-one, I was a strong, determined young woman and not easily persuaded by a guy who thought he could impress me easily.

"I surely would, if that's what it takes for you to go to lunch with me tomorrow," he answered with a bright, charming smile.

What could it hurt, I thought, *he won't ever drive all the way to New York to see me on a regular basis anyway. Why not have some fun while I'm here?* Besides, he sounded so determined to take me out, it felt good and so I agreed.

To my astonishment he did come to see me that first time and every other weekend for over a year until we got married. I lived at the International YMCA in New York the first time he called. I was having lunch in the dining room when they told me I had a gentleman caller. I rushed to my room, afraid he was going to hang up, but he didn't. He even agreed to let me make all the arrangements for the weekend of our first real date and all the ones after that. I made sure to tell him, though, he would have to stay at a hotel about three minutes away since I could not receive a gentleman in my room. Even that didn't deter him and soon our romance began.

I went back to my chair and the wonderful memories of our life together helped me to stop crying. I got up and decided to wash my tear stained face. As I reached to turn the faucet on, I looked in the mirror. I wasn't twenty-one anymore, but the years had been kind to me. In my forties, I didn't have gray hair yet and while no longer a size seven, my figure had held up pretty well. Allen had always loved my eyes. When we dated, he called them deep, liquid pools he liked to get lost in. Although right now, they looked red and swollen from crying, it was still nice to remember his silly, romantic talk from way back.

I walked back into the bedroom and stood in front of the bed. *I can't sleep in the chair, I have to go to bed, it's late. Tomorrow will be a busy day.*

An hour later I was still awake, thinking about Micah. Our wonderful son was only seventeen. How could he possibly cope with this? We had a joke in the family, if Allen would ever leave, Micah would go with his Dad; they were that close. He was a lot like Allen, a little more laid back and at 5"5' not as tall, but always the life of the party, filled with energy and laughter in his easy going ways. He loved to play basketball and soccer, which gave him a muscular build. Since he went to Cedar Grove Christian Academy and attended church with us, he learned to love the Lord early on.

I will never forget when Allen's brother Bill and I picked him up from his job yesterday at the fast food restaurant. He had been so proud that morning when he left, because they had asked him to work the grill alone for the first time. I did not have the heart to tell him as he talked non-stop on the way to the hospital about how well he had done. Instead, I looked at him with deep sorrow in my heart, knowing his happiness would turn into sadness in just a few minutes. Somehow I wanted to prolong these innocent moments of a young man's excitement over his first job. All too soon we arrived at the hospital.

"I'll race you to Dad's room, Mom," he joked as we got to the ward. I had asked the doctor to leave Allen in the room until Micah could get there.

"Wait, Micah, I have something to tell you," I shouted after him just before he opened the door. I walked toward him with a heavy heart and took his hands. "Micah, Baby, your Dad died this morning."

He stared at me in disbelief for the longest time until he finally managed to say in a thick voice,

"What are you talking about, Mom?"

"I am so sorry, Baby, your Dad is gone."

I watched the shock spread across his face as he finally realized what I had said. Without a word he opened the door and stood at Allen's body. Just like I had done, he stroked his face and then started to cry, the tears streaming down his face. I did not know what to say or how to make it easier for him, and began to cry as well.

Finally, Micah turned to me and with the saddest expression I had ever seen and said,

"Mom, could I talk to Dad alone?"

"Of course, Baby, take your time," I said. "I will wait outside for you."

As I sat in the hallway, Allen's brother Bill came and joined me. He was taller than Allen, very thin, with much lighter skin tone and thin nose and lips. I liked him. He was a kind, gentle man, highly intelligent with a Master Degree in Education from Temple University. He had a wonderful gentleness about him that comforted me as he sat next to me in his quiet, yet strong way.

"Have you called your parents, Ethel?" he asked quietly.

"No, I need to do that as soon as I get home."

Just as Micah came out of the room, a jogging friend of Allen's came up to us to ask how Allen was doing. Ignoring the question, Micah collapsed on the chair next to me and started sobbing so pitifully, it broke my heart.

No one spoke during the ride home from the hospital. The thought that the family would be here soon comforted me. At least for a little while I would not be alone.

My oldest brother John was the first to arrive that evening with his wife Pauline. He held me tight without many words. He and Pauline, a quiet, shy person, only lived fifteen minutes away. She hugged me and asked if she could stay with me over night.

"What happened?" John finally asked as we sat down at the dining room table. We cried together as I told him.

When Micah came in, he took him in his arms and said in a low voice, "I am so sorry about your Dad. I'm here for you, buddy."

I felt better with family around.

My sister Jean and her husband Raymond came shortly thereafter. The minute they walked in, I ran up to Jean and into her arms, crying. She was younger than I and we looked very much alike. She wore her hair pulled back, which showed off her friendly face and ready smile.

"Where is Micah?" she asked.

"I think he is in his room. Why don't you go see him, it would make me feel better, Sis."

The rest of the evening is a blur with the Pastor and his wife coming after the special 'Mortgage burning service' was over. The house was suddenly filled with countless church members, who had followed him from the church.

When everyone had finally left, I felt alone with only Micah in his room. Sleep did not come as my mind was filled with thoughts of Allen's home going service. I could not imagine him in that coffin and me being a widow now. It made me sob into my pillow way into the night, being careful not to let Micah hear me cry.

It was strange, the idea that I could turn to the Lord never came to me. Had I only known that night how He would help me in the days to come, I would have run to Him right then instead of trying to handle everything on my own.

"My flesh and my heart may fail, but God is the strength of my heart and my portion forever." Psalm 73:26

Chapter 2

Why Lord?

𝕴 woke up early the next morning. I looked over where Allen was supposed to be and a crushing feeling of profound sadness and loneliness came over me. It was all true, he was gone! He would always be gone, forever. The thought choked me and I had to sit up to breathe. It was strange, I had imagined at times we might get a divorce, like so many people among our friends, but it had never occurred to me, either one of us could die. Well, maybe when we got real old, but not now. This happened to other people, not to us. He was so full of life and energy; it was hard to imagine he was lying at the undertakers waiting to be cremated. I cringed. What a horrible thought being burned up by fire! It was unimaginable and filled me with panic, until I forced myself to realize, he didn't feel anything, because he was dead.

Dead, it sounded so final and it made me cry, whether for myself or for Allen, I did not know. Why would God be so cruel to take him? The words of my pastor came to me,

"We do not understand the ways of the Lord, all we can do is accept what happens and go on."

He is so right and understood about grief, because he had lost his first wife, I thought.

Immediately, I felt guilty for being so angry. I loved my pastor, he was a good man who cared for the people in his church. I loved his charismatic, outgoing personality and the way he made time for everyone. It was hard to believe he was ever a postal worker.

My mind wondered as I lay there. I wanted to blame God, but I didn't dare. Then my thoughts turned to Allen. *How could you leave me? Who is going to rake the leaves or fix the lawnmower?* The anger in me rose up suddenly. *How dare you leave me now? We were going to go on a vacation to Boston in June. What about that cruise you promised me for our 20th anniversary in December? You broke your promise and now it will never happen. Nothing good will ever happen again with me all alone. I haven't been alone in twenty years. How am I supposed to handle everything that has to be done today, since I have never been in this place before?* I felt overwhelmed and wanted to crawl under the covers and just cry for the rest of the day. I lay very still and tried to pretend none of this had happened and I would wake up and find Allen next to me, grinning his familiar grin.

The anger left as suddenly as it came. How silly to be angry with someone who had died. *But then again, Allen is up there with the Lord having a good time, while I am down here having to do things I have never done before. All those people coming! In a way it was good. They would give me comfort, because they are my brothers and sisters in the Lord and will stand by me and allow me to cry when I feel like it. Mom would be there! I couldn't wait for her to walk through the door, slender, dressed in a nice dress with a hat to match and her large brown eyes looking at me with such love. It would make everything better.*

I decided not to put make-up on while getting dressed that morning. I would just cry again when everybody came and mess it up. How silly to worry about a thing like that; nobody would care.

I was grateful that most of the neighbors had come by last night. Some stopped in because they saw the cars and wanted to know if we were having a party. *Maybe I'm not near as alone as I thought.*

"Ethel, are you awake?" It was my church sister Trudy. She stayed the night and had promised to help me with the preparations of the home going.

"I will stay with you and walk with you through this," she had said with her beautiful, warm and affectionate smile. In her forties, she was attractive, with a strong voice and a self-confidence I envied. She was divorced with one son and worked for the Federal Government. In spite of her job, she was tireless as a church home missionary, teaching Sunday school, setting up the communion table and working with the youth. She had been a close friend for years and I called her by her last name, Keasley.

"I am awake, come on in," I called out.

"The tea is ready and you need some breakfast, girl," she said with a cheerful voice. "It's going to be a busy day, no staying in bed this morning." She stood by the door, waiting for me to get up. When I did, she turned and said, "Come, we'll have a cup of tea in the kitchen and talk before everybody gets here." With that, she headed for the kitchen without waiting for me.

"You will get through this, Ethel," she said as we sat down together at the small table. "The Lord will help you and so will everybody else around here. You have a great family and good neighbors, not to mention the church people."

Her voice seemed far away. I felt detached from reality somehow, because I heard what she said, but it didn't penetrate. *How am I going to get through this day?*

"How are you coping, Ethel?" she finally asked in a gentle tone.

"I don't know, Keasley, I can't believe he's gone. My mind doesn't want to accept it." I took a sip of tea. "Nothing seems real and I am convinced he's going to come walking through the front door, telling me it was all a joke."

"I can only imagine how you feel. It was all so unexpected. Who would've thought that a simple hernia operation would do this." She looked at me thoughtfully, "We never know when our time comes, because our life doesn't belong to us. The Lord decides when it runs out and all we can do is accept it." She put her hand on mine in a loving gesture. "You'll just have to make due with us now, won't you?"

"I haven't really talked to God since it happened, Keasley. I wanted to get angry with Him, but I don't dare, but don't ask me to thank Him for taking my Allen either." I started to cry again. "Why did He do that? It isn't fair. What have I ever done to deserve this? I have always gone to church and served Him, why did He take him?" I was sobbing.

Keasley sat quietly and let me cry. I was faced with one of those moments when we rail against God, not out of rebellion and disbelief, but out of pain and loss. I knew intellectually the Lord understood and loved me anyway, but I didn't feel it in my heart. What I did feel was, He had allowed this to happen and could have stopped it. Why didn't He? I realized there was no good answer and that made it even worse. Some family and friends who had come over yesterday or had talked to me on the phone, gave me the worn-out phrases that I had used many times myself when someone had died. 'He is in a better place' or 'God knows what He's doing and has something better planned for you'. And then there is the one that says, 'The best is yet to come'. The list is endless. None of them help, because they don't know and neither do I why God does what He does.

To know and accept the plan of God when tragedy strikes is impossible for our mind to grasp or agree with, because at the time it goes against everything we want or could possibly understand. It causes a feeling of helplessness and abandonment, envisioning endless days of loneliness stretching out in front of us like a dry, parched dessert that reaches beyond the horizon of the future.

No words, no action and no explanation can penetrate those feelings, except maybe for a moment, because they have a way of coming back as sudden as a dam breaking in the middle of the night. As a Christian, we are expected to accept God's will cheerfully and with joy. Instead, it sounds almost cruel when someone quotes the scripture that says in James 1:2,

"Consider it all joy, my brethren, when you encounter various trials."

One thing I learned during that time, scripture can be like a battering ram for our soul if it is used while too wounded to accept or understand it. It took me a long time before I could believe that God's word is always true, even in this, but I couldn't see it right then. It is the Holy Spirit who soothes and heals in time, gently, gradually and without condemnation.

What is it then I wanted and needed to hear from those who came to comfort me? At the time I had no idea, but looking back, I yearned to be reassured that things will be alright and the Lord will be there with me. He and those around me will love and understand when I don't have the faith to believe, act and speak as a mature Christian in every situation. I wanted to be loved in spite of my doubts and fears by those who love me. It does not always need words to express it, just a smile, a hug or a card, given without a sermon or quoting scripture can be more than enough.

The hardest thing to endure is, when someone tries to console a grieving person by recounting an incident which tops what happened to them. It belittles your grief and makes the one sharing feel superior in their suffering.

To truly comfort someone means to forget about ourselves and concentrate on their tragedy. Our own experience can help us to show compassion and understanding for the one who is hurting without sharing it. There are, however, times when they can be of help, just not during the initial few days of grief.

To use the phrase, 'I understand', when we have never been in their shoes, is a thoughtless statement. To honestly admit that we have never had someone close to us die, is not only more honest, but shows genuine feelings for their circumstances. In order to have compassion, it is not necessary for us to have been through the same type of tragedy, but it takes unconditional love and sincere compassion for the one grieving.

One of the worst things someone can do is to blame the person who died for their death. For example, if he had smoked and died of lung cancer, it does no good to bring that up during the time of initial grieving. As a matter of fact, it is never a good time to mention it, because it involves judgment and condemnation. One of the most astounding remarks came from a well-meaning person in my church after the funeral.

"You are probably better off."
After walking away angry, I realized, she had decided, since Allen hadn't come to church regularly lately, he was no longer a good enough husband and Christian for me. At that time, I walked away in anger, but today I realize, if God treated us that way, none of us, including her, would be able to stand before Him.

I hope today I would pray for her with understanding in the words of Jesus, "Father forgive them, for they know not what they do." (Luke 23:24)

Many of the above mentioned things, while quite inappropriate at this initial phase, can be helpful much later after God has soothed the terrible wounds of loss and grief. That is also when scripture can be like a healing ointment to our soul by showing God's love and compassion through His Word.

To give advice, correction or quote scripture in times of tragedy, should only be done by someone who truly knows and loves the one they are talking to. In most cases, it would be much better to pray for the person in private and allow God to choose the right person to speak for Him, since the one He chooses knows the circumstance in the situation. Giving advice or criticize with only partial knowledge, can do a lot of damage by wounding a hurting soul even more than it already is. Many times it is much more helpful to listen rather than talk and show compassion rather than judgment when being in the presence of the ones left behind. To give advice at this time sounds more like judgment, while allowing *them* the freedom to talk will bring relief in their sorrow.

"Mercy triumphs over judgement." James 2:13

Chapter 3

Love in the midst of the Storm

𝕸 icah came into the kitchen quietly. He had been strangely silent since that first outburst of grief at the hospital. I was worried and tried to talk to him, but with no success. He stayed in his room and I had no idea what he was doing or what was going through his mind. It made me feel helpless and frustrated. It felt like I had not just lost a husband, but a son as well.

"Honey, is there anything I can get you to eat?" Keasley asked him. "I fixed some eggs and bacon and can make you toast to go with it," she added as she walked to the stove.

"That would be good, Sister Keasley," Micah said. "I'll take it to my room. He turned to me, "Mom, Frankie is coming over later. We're going to hang out together after school."

"That sounds great, Baby," I answered. "I have to make arrangements at the Undertaker's later on when Pastor Morris gets here."

Frankie's father had died just two days ago and I didn't know if it was good or bad for him to be with Micah so soon after his own loss. He was Micah's best friend and they attended the same school. Frankie was taller than Micah, more muscular and one of the best basketball and football players at Cedar Grove Christian Academy; good enough to be in the running for a draft pick by a major team. I was glad he was coming over and the two might be able to help each other deal with their grief. Frankie's father had had cancer and had not been expected to live, and I was worried it might be too much for him to deal with the added burden of my son.

Micah took the plate Keasley fixed him and went back to his room. Watching him leave, I felt somewhat rejected that he did not seem to need me at a time like this; but just for a fleeting moment. He had his way of dealing with this and I had mine. We both felt too much pain to be of any help to each other and so turned to our friends instead. Keasley had offered to make all the necessary phone calls and help me write the death announcement cards. She was also organizing the home going service and type the program once the date was set.

After we were finished with breakfast, four ladies from our block came to the door to ask what they could do to help. Keasly suggested they could be in charge of the food during the next few days here at the house. It made me feel good to know so many people came forward to help in such a short time. It also spoke volumes for Kealey's organizational talents.

Suddenly, the doorbell rang. It was Pastor Ernest Morris, his wife Winifred and Chaplain Elmer Hunter. The moment they walked in, I broke down and cried,

"I am so scared, what am I going to do? Please, help me, Pastor." It felt good to know others were taking charge of everything that had to be done, something I could not do at this point. Pastor Morris was not just a wonderful pastor but a good friend. He and his wife would take responsibility where I had no idea what to do about the service, the music and all those things that needed to be organized. He was of middle age with a kind face and an outgoing, friendly demeanor. His small, lively eyes behind large, rimless glasses were filled with compassion as he listened to my plea for help. His strong, steady voice made me feel safe, as he said the very words I needed to hear.

"We are here for you, Ethel, you know that, day and night, Winifred and I are ready to help in any way we can." He looked at me with his wonderful, warm smile and added, "The Lord is always with you, you know that, don't you? You draw near to Him and He will draw near to you, just like He says in His Word."

"Why did He take my Allen, Pastor?" I cried. "I can't live without him." I was sobbing again. "This is so hard and I don't know what to do."

"You don't have to know what to do, child, the Lord will guide you and lead you every minute of every day," Winifred said. She was a powerful woman of God, strong in faith and with a sure manner that calmed me down. She was a strikingly beautiful lady, exuding a large presence about her. Her intelligent eyes, smooth skin and perfect, white teeth gave her face a look of confidence mixed with genuine kindness and love as she spoke those words to me; and I believed her.

A large part of the afternoon was taken up by making arrangements with the undertaker. Pastor Morris and Chaplain Hunter took me there and helped me finalize a date for the going home service. By the time we got back, neighbors and friends from the church had brought enough food to feed everyone lunch.

During the day, in spite of the many people who came and went, I noticed Micah was still in his room. When I finally found a moment to check on him, he was on the computer, quiet and withdrawn. I realized he was waiting for his friend Frankie. Again, I felt a stab of rejection. Why did he not want or need me right now? A wave of loneliness washed over me and I longed for my mother to get here. It is strange, we are all still children when it comes to our mothers, no matter how old we get.

Micah had asked if he could pick out the suit for Allen. I realized this was important to him, sort of the last thing he could ever do for his beloved father.

Queen Esther Smith, that was her name, was of small stature, but a giant in the eyes of each of her twelve children. There was no doubt she was the matriarch of the family, filled with godly wisdom and unconditional love for us. In our minds, there was nothing Mama couldn't fix, couldn't make us feel better about or fill us with the knowledge that God loved us and we were special in His eyes. I always thought I was her favorite, but today I have a sneaking suspicion, she made every one of us feel the same.

Dad couldn't come, because he was too sick. I am sure it was hard on him not to be there for me. He was a gentle man, who had faithfully provided for his family until his children were grown. He was a quiet, wonderful father, who loved his wife, his Queen. Mama may have been the strong one, but I have a feeling, the two of them in their private moments, were as close as any two people could be. There was a calm assurance in their relationship, a stability that we children knew would always be there and it gave us a feeling of security and love while we were growing up. We may not have been rich, but there was no doubt, we grew up in an environment with the kind of wealth money couldn't buy.

When Mama finally arrived, I was overjoyed and flew into her arms with tears of relief. Now all would be well. Even Micah came out and hugged her, crying. I know her strong faith would carry Micah and I through this. With her favorite phrase, 'Live and be blessed', she had a way of setting things right in my life over the years. I felt comforted as she whispered it in my ears while she held me close. She exuded an aura of faith, strength and hope as she put her arms around me; and for a moment the confusion and feelings of abandonment of the last days evaporated in her embrace. She was Mom, the rock we all looked to in good times and bad.

Over the rest of the day, most of my siblings arrived. Some would not arrive until the home going service. I felt enveloped in their love and encouraging words, although it did nothing to help with the pain that filled my heart every time I stopped to think that Allen was gone.

There was a steady stream of church people and neighbors who came with their love offering tucked in a card. I will always cherish those cards, because they showed their love and caring attitude in a way that ministered to me greatly.

On the other hand, some of them, at a loss of what to say, spoke those well-meaning phrases or tried to tell me about God's will and shared that Allen was in a better place. They did not understand that during these first days of grieving, I did not want to hear about God's will or Allen having left me for a better place. What could be better than him being with me?

Somehow, there is a desire in people to stop a grieving person from grieving through these remarks. While it makes *them* feel better, these phrases deny the grieving person the time and opportunity to let grief run its course. Acknowledging what happened helps much more. Encouragement to bypass these emotions actually causes discomfort and makes us feel that we wouldn't have them if we were a better Christian. It puts an additional burden on the grieving person and one they are not able to handle during this time.

Friends, family and neighbors need to understand that at this initial time there are no words adequate enough to comfort anyone. A loving smile, a gesture or the gentle assurance that they will be there is enough. To share a happy story or memory about the lost loved one helps the grieving person to laugh and forget the pain and loss for an instance. It is this normal behavior in others that allows them to be themselves and show their hurt and pain while laughing at happy memories.

The strain to live up to other's expectations during this time can become too much, since it takes enormous effort to put on a front of faith, spirituality and calm that is simply not there. Especially well-meaning Christian friends, who have never experienced the loss of a loved one, have a tendency to fall into this trap of telling others how they should handle grief instead of allowing them to show and experience it in their own way.

Everyone handles grief differently, but no one can ignore it or bury it under super spiritual platitudes that are neither true nor real. For it is the freedom to feel and express what is in our hearts without the disapproval of others, that helps us deal with our own feelings.

Knowing that neither God nor friends expect us to be filled with faith and joy about what happened, is a tremendous relief during this time. Letting the bereaved know that the Lord understands and waits patiently until their grief has run its course before He expects them to be able to 'count it all joy when various trial come upon me", helps them to see His love in a more real way.

In a little booklet by RBC Ministries it states, "There are many advantages to being a Christian, but the absence of pain is not one of them". Pain is the way to let us know that something is wrong with our soul. To ignore it, is not only wrong, but can be detrimental. To acknowledge it and allow it time to heal with God's love, is called the grieving process and takes time even for the most mature Christian.

Pain and sorrow are a harsh reality of life in this sin-fallen world. They can bring anger, doubt and fear toward God or people at the onset, until our mind and soul are ready to deal with them properly. Those around us can help with the initial shock by simply being there and feeling the pain with us, sharing the doubt and anger at what happened, without expecting us to be giants of faith.

Think of it as sitting in a little tent in the middle of nowhere during a terrible storm. Your friends can stand outside telling you not to fear or they can join you by holding your hand and wait for the storm to blow over without blaming you for being afraid. Compassion is feeling what I feel and still loving me without expectation or reproach until I can feel as clearly about what happened as they do.

There is no formula to tell us what to say during times like this, since everybody grieves in different ways. Some people need to be alone during this time, others want to be surrounded by friends and family. We need to allow each person their own way of grieving without feeling rejected or left out. Let them decide freely how to deal with their feelings, especially in the very first few days. All you can do is be there for them and then let them tell you what they need from you instead of you telling them what they should do.

This was especially true as Micah was unable to come to me for comfort, but turned to his friend Frankie instead. It took quite a while before the two of us were able to share our grief together and make us feel the closeness I had longed for during the first days.

When tragedy strikes, instead of bringing us closer to our loved ones, it sometimes can tear us apart. Many marriages have broken up after a child dies, not because the parents blamed each other, but each was unable to be there for the other, because they were too filled with pain. In other words, each had no empty spot left in their heart to take on more of the other's sorrow.

Micah felt unable to comfort me, because his heart was filled with such intolerable grief, he had nothing left to give. He did not reject me, but turned to Frankie who had room left in his heart to understand and feel what he felt. It was not a lack of love for me, but a lack of room to accommodate my grief on top of his. When that happens, it is imperative that we find a friend like Frankie for Micah and Keasley, for me. Both of us instinctively reached out for someone to help bear our grief.

If we withdraw and try to handle this sorrow by ourselves, divorce happens or even thoughts of suicide can enter our minds. There are simply some things we cannot and should not handle alone, because we are usually unable to reach out to the Lord during this initial stage. This has nothing to do with lack of faith, but with the inability to think clearly and rationally to know and understand that pain will lessen someday and there will be a future.

By turning to my friend Keasley, I was able to share my feelings and fears, my memories and yes, even my lack of faith, knowing she would understand. The Lord used her to help me find the way back to Him when I was blind with grief. He used Frankie to do the same for Micah until both of us had enough faith to help each other as time went on.

**"Blessed are those who mourn, for they will be comforted.
Matthew 5:4**

Chapter 4

Going Home

The funeral, or home going as we call it, was an event that gave both Micah and I a sense of closure. The church was packed with people from Allen's and my work, Micah's school friends and our church family as well as Allen's family. Allen always said he hated to go to these things, but he would have been astounded to see and hear the send-off he got as people shared the love they had for him and for those who he left behind.

In my culture, a home going, by its very name, is a celebration of having been promoted to eternal glory with the Lord. In spite of the sadness, there is this Christian hope and joy at the thought of having made it to 'the other side' and spending the rest of our existence in the presence of God.

Instead of dressing in black and hopelessness, we dress in white and with exuberance we celebrate the transition from this life to a better one, while not forgetting the sorrow that is in our hearts for being left behind.

The one moment that stood out was when I heard the very song I loved and needed to hear. "Can't nobody do me like Jesus". It felt like a love song from the Lord, saying to me, 'I hear you, I see you and got you in the palm of My hand. But most of all, I love you and I will make everything alright.' As I listened, I strongly felt the first sign of my spiritual and emotional recovery had begun as I felt a peace come over me for the first time since Allen died. I will treasure this memory forever, because that is when I knew the Lord was with me and would always be there. Enveloped in the midst of friends and family, Micah and I felt the love and compassion of those who came to offer it freely with song, testimonials and praise to the Lord for His goodness.

The pastor spoke words of comfort, encouragement and hope. My heart was made glad for the love and support that surrounded us during this time.

Micah had written some wonderful words about his dad that touched my heart.

A- Always
L- loving his family
L- living for Christ
E- entering heaven
N- never forsaking God
   or his family

P- Pursuing
E- Loving his family
R- Rising to the occasion
K- Keeping God's Word
I- in his heart
N- Needing/giving love
S- Saved by God

It is amazing, how one song, one word spoken in love or one thought from the Lord brought the beginning of healing, even at a funeral. I allowed myself to be carried away in the comfort and blessing from the Lord and the many people who came.

The actual burial was early the next morning. It was a beautiful day, much too bright and sunny for a sad day like this I thought. There was such a feeling of finality when I watched the casket being lowered into the ground. The reality of my Allen's body being swallowed up by the earth was almost too much to bear. It so helped me to know that it was only the empty shell of his body that remained, because his spirit was with the Lord. And it came to me, how do people who are not believers, cope with the thought of death? It is even worse for those who are left behind to think they are gone forever, vanished as if they never existed.

Hope, and the joy of seeing Allen again in the presence of our Lord Jesus Christ flooded my mind. I suddenly felt peace and comfort in the sure knowledge of faith in a God who sent His Son to die for Allen and me so that we can spend eternity together in the presence of the Lord.

My thoughts were interrupted by a most awful sound. It was supposed to be taps played by a young man from the Veterans Department who wanted to honor Allen. With all his good intentions, he was so overcome by emotions, what was supposed to be this hauntingly beautiful music, came out as a hauntingly, horrible mismatch of wrong notes. Micah leaned over to me and whispered,

"I know Dad is truly dead, because if not, he would have taken that horn away from him."

It was astounding, God can use anything to help with our grief. In the midst of our deepest sorrow, Micah and I had to laugh as we could imagine Allen walking up to the man and just grabbing it away from him with a funny remark. It broke the sadness and gloom in our hearts and replaced it with laughter. What a wonderful God we serve! As I looked around to see what people would think when they saw us laugh, I realized they were smiling as well. I truly hope the young man was not aware of his 'painful' performance, otherwise I would have told him how it cheered us up in spite of it all.

Since the burial was early on Saturday, the re-pass, held at the church, was a breakfast with all the trimmings. The ladies had outdone themselves with their fine cooking. I was pleased to see over a hundred people sitting at the many tables or standing with a plate in their hands, talking and remembering Allen, while enjoying to see each other.

It felt wonderful to see my whole family from Alabama, Allen's folks from Philadelphia, as well, as well as my friends and neighbors all standing with Micah and me during this difficult time. It was as if they shielded me from the crushing loneliness and anguish over my loss and helped me to make it through the worst, painful first few days without breaking down.

Especially, having my mother and my siblings there was tremendously comforting. There is something about family that gives us strength and security during this time. Maybe it is the memory of childhood and the idea that we belong together. It is the thought, that no matter how old we are or how far apart we live, we are still a unit, molded and bonded during childhood with Mom and Dad as the anchor that holds us together.

I was very fortunate to have had wonderful parents. I remember my mother as she taught us during the summer, when all the other kids were running free. We had to do 'homework' every day. She decided that we should not forget what we had learned during school. Both of my parents instilled in us the wonderful values that are so lacking in our society today, honesty, decency and reliance on the Lord. It is a great accomplishment to have raised twelve children without even one of them going down the wrong path. Mind you, there were a few scrapes, but all in all, every one of us loves the Lord and grew into men and women my parents can be proud of.

A funeral or going home service is not *for* the one who died, but more so *about* them. It is a tradition in our society to let those who are left behind know how much everyone cared. This helps the entire community to share their grief with the family of losing one of their own. Death is not a subject people like to talk about. Even at funerals we try very hard not to use the word dead or dying. 'Gone to be with the Lord', 'departed', 'gone to a better place', and 'left this earth' are only a few of the phrases used to circumvent the simple truth that someone died.

The fear of death is present in all of us and is mainly designed as a defense mechanism to avoid places or things that could kill us. While there are a few who leave this life voluntarily, most of us are hoping to live to a ripe old age and we do everything in our power to get there. And yet, for Christians, death is a promotion from an existence filled with struggle and strife to a promise of eternal bliss. So why is it so hard for most of us to come to terms with death?

It is the ultimate test of faith. It is the one time we have to make a decision whether we know there is a God; and if there is, did He really send His Son Jesus to die for us so we can spend eternity with Him? Yet it is that tiny doubt that confronts us during this time, namely, is God real and does He know how hard it is that He took my loved one? Is there really life after death?

For me, this was the ultimate test of trust. How can I manage alone? Will I have enough strength, courage and wisdom to care for Micah by myself? Will God supply all my needs like He promises, knowing Jesus never had to pay bills or pay the mortgage or felt lonely and scared of the future. Well, maybe He did when He told Peter to find money in the fish's mouth to pay taxes.

It is the ultimate test of love. Does God really love me? Does He even know I exist and if He does, will He love me even when I fail? In the middle of the night, when I lay there, heartbroken and without hope, will I still be able to love Him or will I give up and turn away from Him and try to manage on my own?

These are the questions we all have to face during this time of loss and grief. Mankind has asked them throughout the ages when life ceases and we are confronted by the finality of death.

Has God ever answered them?

Faith is not based on feelings or emotions, but on a firm decision to trust a loving God who tells me in His Word that He loves me and will never leave me nor forsake me.

"No, in all these things we are more than conquerors through him who loves us. For I am convinced that neither death nor life, neither angels nor demons, neither the present nor the future, nor any powers, neither height nor depth, not anything else in all creation, will be able to separate us from the love of God that is in Christ Jesus." Romans 8:37-39

In the past there were times when I read the Bible out of habit, obligation or because it was expected of me. When I was faced with overpowering loss, I needed much stronger assurance from the Lord, knowing that He knew I was hurting and that He would be with me. It is this state of desperation that brought a closeness with God I had not been able to experience before. That is when the decision to believe turned into feelings of peace and trust. We listen to the words in church and think we know what faith is. Not until I was walking through the valley of the shadows of death did I experience that He was with me, because it was then that I did not just believe in God, but I BELIEVED HIM. There is a big difference.

All of us want to live on the mountain top in our walk with the Lord, thinking that is where we grow and mature. Have you looked at the peak of a high mountain? There is nothing but solid rock. If I stayed there, I would starve to death. It is in the valley where the rich pasture is that brings nourishment to my soul. And yes, it is in the valley where I encounter trials and tribulation, but the Shepherd is with me and will carry me on His shoulders if necessary.

Let Him carry you during this time when you don't have the strength to walk. Allow Him to comfort you with His wonderful Word when you are unable to speak; and let Him guide you when you cannot see where you are going.

"In the same way, the Spirit helps us in our weakness. We do not know what we ought to pray for, but the Spirit himself intercedes for us with groans that words cannot express. And he who searches our hearts knows the mind of the Spirit, because the Spirit intercedes for the saints in accordance with God's will. (Romans 8:26-27)

When words fail you and even reading His Word will not bring peace, try to sit and listen for His voice. Praying is another way of having a relationship with God. It does not have to be a one-way conversation, where you do all the talking and He does the listening. Try to be still before Him and you will see that His small, still voice will be there to give you exactly the reassurance you need, the help you are looking for and the love you so desperately want to feel at just that moment.

But if you still cannot reach out to Him, reach out to someone who can do it for you, a friend, your pastor or a neighbor. Tell them you do not know how to talk to God. And do not feel ashamed, the Lord already knows it and your friend will understand.

"Be still and know that I am God." (Psalm 46:10)

Chapter 5

When the Pain is too much

To be blessed with a strong support system is one of the best ways to deal with the first days of grief. I will never forget the many people from my family, my church, my neighborhood and the friends that reached out to Micah and me during those early days of grief.

The days after the home going, when those who came from out of town had left, I could have been devastatingly lonely if it hadn't been for my four neighbors, Elouise, Dorothy, Katherine and Carol. Whether planned or not, they managed to make sure I was never alone during that time. With love, tact and goodies they managed to be there with me, which kept me from getting depressed or lonely. Their compassion and help in those days overwhelmed me with gratitude and a feeling of belonging, which was worth more than I could ever repay.

What truly touched me was, when a co-worker named Theresa offered to help me financially until my insurance money came in. I am sure she did not have a lot herself, but was willing to help me. Since Allen had gotten a policy just a few months before he died, the company demanded a lot of proof that his death was not due to a previous condition. It took them from June to the next January before they paid out. This put me in a tight financial dilemma and her help was truly a blessing.

I was amazed at the many people who helped me in countless other ways in those early days. Some of them, like Theresa, would have never come to mind.

My friend Keasley, a single mother, as well as the pastor's sister Alice, a widow, stood by me with prayer, advice and help on how to pay bills, run the house and many other things that were now my responsibility. Allen had done all those things with such efficiency, I never had to worry about them before.

They also made sure I got involved in church by singing in the choir and helping with Bible school. It got me out of the house in the evenings and among friends.

Micah was true to his word when he told me he would take care of me. With his 17 years, he had taken on the role of protector and I allowed him to feel needed in that way. He worked in a flower shop during his last year in high school and I was touched when he brought me flowers several times. In return, I decided to make a date with him one day, during which I could teach him how to treat a girl right when he was ready. I made him open the car door for me, pull out a chair at the restaurant and altogether learn how to act like a gentleman.

Thinking back, it was an amusing time when, talking about how to treat a lady, the subject of sex came up. I told him something my father made sure all of my brothers heard when they started dating, "I don't want no extra people coming up. So keep your pants zipped up."

Micah was mortified and tried to stop me from saying any more, but I was on a roll. *I may never have the chance again,* I thought and continued,

"I think you are handsome, cute and adorable and I love you. So if a girl tells you those things, you tell her your mom already told you. Then you tell her that God has a plan for you and that plan is to stay clean until marriage."

He listened politely, hoping that the conversation was heading in a more neutral direction.

We then talked about college. He was pretty upset he couldn't go to Virginia State with his friend Danny because of our money situation. Since I worked as a dental assistant at Temple University Dental School, his tuition would be free if he attended there. It was hard for him to give up the plans that had seemed so sure not too long ago.

During a visit to Allen's family a few weeks later, Micah and I experienced a wonderful, strong, committed support group as we spent the holiday together. It helped us both to overcome Allen's death as they showed their love in countless kind gestures.

In times of grief, one of the most important help is family or a good support system made up of church people, friends or neighbors. We are not just made in God's image, but we are also designed for fellowship with others. That goes especially during hard times. That is why the Lord said 'Where two or three are gathered, there I am in the midst of you'. We are not meant to carry our joys or sorrows alone. Imagine, you won a million dollars in the lottery; the first thing any of us would think of is with whom we can share the good news? It is this desire for sharing our joy or sorrow, success or failure with those we love that helps us experience and deal with the good, the bad and the ugly in daily living. That is also why God said after He created Adam, "It is not good for man to be alone". He understood that by design we need others to live a fulfilled life by sharing with those around us the blessings and sorrows that come our way.

And yet, many times when tragedy strikes, we want to crawl in a hole and never come out, because we cannot bear the thought of being with anyone. There are many reasons for withdrawing from others.

Sometimes we cannot find the words, sort out our feelings or stand the pain of what happened, least of all share these things with others.

Another, we are afraid others don't understand or feel the depth of our sorrow.

The third is, what if people say the wrong thing and the pain gets worse.

The fourth, we might be unable to share our feelings, even our guilt or shame over why our loved one died. Communication during the first stages of grief is difficult for everyone, because of the multitude of strong emotions and feelings in our heart.

And yet another, what if I don't act spiritual enough by crying or, God forbid, feeling anger toward the loved one or even God when the need to show faith and a 'stiff upper lip' is more than I can bear right now. So if I stay away from people, I can let my feelings out without being judged by anyone.

Financial worries are especially hard to share during this time. There is no way I can share this embarrassing subject with anyone right now. What kind of a cold, worldly person would I be, thinking of money at a time like this?

One of the biggest reasons for withdrawing from others is depression. It can range from a few days to years of sorrow and pain. To feel depressed can cause us to be overwhelmed, sad, hopeless, angry and listless, among other things. These feelings can be so strong, they color our outlook on life and hinder us from ever getting passed the first stages of grief. Instead of healing gradually, the wound of our loss bleeds for weeks, months and even years.

If you are in this situation, I would advise you to seek medical help, because such prolonged, intense grief is destructive to your soul and body.

There are other reasons, of course, but they all have one thing in common; the enemy wants to isolate us so we cannot let the Lord or others help us with the confusion, fear, anger, grief, helplessness, and the many other feelings that wash over us when loss happens. Then we concentrate on the negative and are incapable of seeing anything positive for our life now or in the future. We become overwhelmed by endless pain and sorrow. Our minds, telling us loneliness and despair is all there is or ever will be, convinces us that we are without hope, faith and love if there is no one to tell us otherwise.

To join a grief support group is a great alternative if you do not have family or friends to stand by you in the long run. When things get 'back to normal', they will return to their lives and you will be expected to cope. When you join a grief group, you will discover that others have gone through the same grief you have. It is a relief to hear about their failures and trials, as well as their successes in building a new life with new goals and directions. We are not an island unto ourselves, but we are people who need others who can relate to us where we are or have been. What a joy to find out we are not alone in our grief and the occasional feelings of deep sorrow which can come out of nowhere and is perfectly normal.

There is one other reason for isolation, and this is probably the most confusing and painful, causing untold rejection and even estrangement with those we love the most.

As I shared before, in the first days of deep trauma and sorrow, Micah and I were unable to communicate our true feelings for each other, since both of us had more than enough to handle with our own grief. This happens often when parents lose a child. Our heart is only so big and can hold only so much grief. Micah and I had lost the one person we both loved the most in our lives and were unable to take on the other's feelings of grief. Instead of holding on to each other, we did the only thing we could do, we turned to our friends who had room in their hearts to take on our feelings. I had my friends Keasley, Alice and Carol, while Micah turned to his friend Frankie.

It may sound strange, but it is quite common for people to get a divorce after they have gone through a trauma. Not because they don't love each other anymore, but they could not understand the rejection of their spouse during this time. Just like I felt rejection when Micah turned to Frankie instead of to me. But then, why did I turn to my friends instead of Micah? Keasley and Alice for instance had walked this road when their husbands died and I had been there for her them. We had history, friendship and something in common together and I trusted them to help me.

For Micah and I, this estrangement did not last very long, but many people never get over it and feel terribly hurt and rejected by those who they love the most. To be allowed the freedom to grieve by our family and friends in the way that is most comfortable for us, is a blessing from the Lord. He is patient and will wait if we cannot be 'spiritual' right away by trying to present a picture of faith and strength. He allows us, with no ill feelings on His part, to turn to someone else for comfort until the worst is over. He does not judge our love for Him, no matter how long it takes, but waits with love and compassion until we are able to feel His arms around us again. He was there all the time, we just weren't able to sense it. No matter how wonderful our family, friends and neighbors are, in the long run, it is the Lord who will sustain us, love us and provide for us. He is the only One who will lead us into a future, where we can laugh again and be what He has designed us to be until He calls us home.

It is not such a bad thing to imagine what it will be like when, in an instant, you stand before the Lord in all His Glory. Just think, He will welcome you as His beloved son or daughter with a smile that will give you such joy as you cannot ever imagine. And then, wonder of wonders, there are your loved ones standing next to Him and welcoming you with outstretched arms.

That is the hope that makes me different from the world. Here I will have trouble, but it is just for a short time. I have all eternity to spend in the presence of the Lord and the people I love, including my Allen.

"For we are His workmanship, created in Christ Jesus to do good works, which God prepared in advance for us to do."
Ephesians 2:10

Chapter 6

Alone

𝕿 he house was still. It was early in the morning. I laid on the bed with a strange feeling, staring at the ceiling. Everyone had gone home the day before and I felt as if the world had stopped turning. I held my breath. *This is when Allen should be calling.*

"It's time to rise and shine, sleepy head." The day wouldn't be complete without him telling me the same thing every morning, when we both knew I was already up. It was part of our daily routine, his way of telling me how much he loved me. I started sobbing when I realized he would never call again, because he was dead! I would have given anything in the world to hear his voice one more time, telling me one of his silly jokes or teasing me about something that was totally unimportant or just plain ridiculous. *Just one more time, Lord.*

This morning was painfully hard for me and I wished I could have just crawled back under the cover, waiting for the world to start turning again. Normal. That is what I wanted, for my life to return to the way it was. *Why, Lord? Why did You let this happen? All I want is normal, nothing special, just life the way it was when Allen was here. Is that so much to ask? Why would You take him from me, I don't see a reason. I wanted us to grow old together and watch Micah graduate, get a good job and get married. Now Allen will never see his grandchildren or take me on a cruise. The cruise. It would have been so nice to stand on deck of a great ship and hold his hand as we looked out over the waves. We would have gotten some new clothes just for the occasion and looked elegant, pretending we did this sort of thing all the time. Instead, I have to worry about having enough money to get by until the insurance pays. What if they don't? What if they never will and I have to go on welfare and Micah has to quit his school just when he has only one more year to go? What if I lose the house and have to move in with Mom? Then I would have to give up my job and move away and probably never find another one. And then Micah would be mad at me and stop loving me, because maybe he always loved his dad more than me.*

My world seemed suddenly spinning as a gloomy future paraded before my eyes. Overwhelming fear and anger flooded my heart and I pulled the covers over me tight. *Why did everybody leave me and lived their normal, wonderful lives with their husbands? Why did they not care about me now that the funeral was over? Don't they know how alone I am, how scared and angry? How could I possibly share with anyone how I really feel? They look to me as if I am a strong Christian, able to have faith throughout all this. I don't have any faith, Lord. I feel You took him from me and now I am alone. Micah looks to me to do the right thing. I don't know what the right thing is nor do I care. I just want to die and get it over with. I do not want to be poor and have to rely on people to give me money and food. PLEASE, GOD, HELP ME!*

I lay there perfectly still as these thoughts washed over me like a broken dam. I had no strength to resist them, no energy to get up and take charge of my life. What was the use, without Allen, nothing was the same and never would be.

That's when I heard Micah in the kitchen. Micah! I had to get up and help him face the day before he went to school. *He needs me!*

"How are you this morning, Baby?" I asked, when I entered the kitchen. "Let me fix you some breakfast."

"I can do it, Mom. Let me fix you some. You need to get ready for work; I will have it done in no time." He sounded good, certainly better than I felt. It made me feel ashamed that my son was handling things better than I; what kind of a mother am I? I was glad to have a reason to take a shower so he would not see the bad shape I was in.

It was equally hard at work that day. I tried to sound normal, but didn't quite make it. Everybody was helpful and kind as the day wore on. I had trouble concentrating and made some mistakes. It just added to my depression and fear that I might never be able to do my job and then I would be fired. No matter how hard I tried, I could not shake my worries, and the more I tried to act normal, the worse I got. Finally, when the day was over, I rushed out without saying goodbye and was glad to be alone in my car, because I couldn't hold back the tears any longer. I dreaded going home to an empty house until I remembered Micah. Why did I act like he wasn't there? He needed me and I didn't want him to, because I needed Allen more. *What about me, I need someone to take care of me!* I felt selfish and miserable and wanted to run away to a place where I could find peace. The negative thoughts were still there and I didn't want them, but neither did I know how to stop the merry-go-round of worries, anxiety and fear.

Six months short of twenty years of marriage and I am a widow, the single parent of a teenage son and the head of the household. This is ridiculous! How did I get here, how can I handle all this? I felt overwhelmed, scared, angry, lost and totally unprepared.

God, are you listening to me? I don't hear You or feel You. I bet You are mad at me, because I said I was angry with You. Even if I tell You I'm not, You know it anyway. Are You angry? If You are, I am really lost, because I don't know how not to be right now. Please, help me! Let me feel that You still love me by helping me to stop letting the enemy overwhelm me.

I was parked in the drive way of my house, crying and sobbing, hoping Micah wasn't home yet to see me. Thank goodness, he wasn't and I had time to wash my face and put on a good front by the time he got back from soccer practice.

Nothing helped that day, no word from the Lord, no friends came over and no one called. It was as if the world had forgotten about me, including the Lord. I spent most of the evening sitting in my favorite chair in the bedroom, staring at my open Bible. I tried to read, but my mind could not grasp the words or their meaning. I even tried my favorite scriptures, but even they sounded empty and hollow. I had never felt so totally alone and abandoned.

And then suddenly, a horrible thought came to me. I was the one who had encouraged Allen to have the surgery done earlier than he had planned, because I wanted him to be fully recovered by the time we went on our cruise. It was all my fault! If he had waited like he wanted to, he would still be alive. I sat frozen in horror. I had killed him! My Allen would still be here if I hadn't acted so selfish about that stupid cruise. I couldn't even cry. I had killed him! I knew it wasn't true, but I couldn't shake the thoughts. I realized this was from the enemy, but I was unable to stop him. I also knew, God hadn't stopped loving me, but I had no faith to believe it. God, please help me! Show me somehow that You love me so that I can see it with my eyes, hear it with my ears and feel it in my soul. Let me know I am not this horrible person who helped kill her husband. My mind went blank and I was without feelings of any kind, except a terrible, heavy weariness throughout my body. With extreme effort I got up and went to bed and was grateful for sleep.

When negative thoughts come in like a flood, nothing seems to be able to stop them. On those days we feel abandoned, forsaken and utterly tossed around like a ragdoll in the midst of a whirlwind. Faith is far removed and hope non-existent. It feels like a storm best waited out with no resistance so it will pass sooner. The storm in our mind is our soul trying to cope and sort out what happened and bring order into our thinking. Like in any storm, the aftermath shows the full destruction, laid out openly for everyone to see, except us, because we are too confused and stunned to take it in.

Think of your mind as a place with many drawers orderly arranged. When tragedy strikes, the event pulls them all out and throws them on a heap in total disarray. To put them back in order, we go through a whirlwind of confusion and frustration and stare at them in anger and fear, because we may not be able to remember where they are supposed to go.

The mind is a wonderful thing, created by God, to go through a process which works perfectly well if we allow it time to put order back where it was lost.

This is called the grieving process. While it works differently with everyone, there are certain paths it takes to bring order out of the chaos in our mind. Whether we are a Christian or not, this process is necessary and cannot be hurried or ignored. It is, however, greatly helped if we have the Lord to guide us, love us and help us during this time. Only He can sustain us with a hope of seeing our loved ones again. And it is this hope that will bring healing and order to our mind, soul and spirit. For without hope there is no future and no healing. Without His promise of eternal life there is nothing but death for the one we lost and in the end, for us.

But it sometimes takes a while to remember His promises in the midst of the turmoil. On that day, I definitely couldn't feel anything other than negative emotions. How I wish I could have had more faith, for in the days to come, the Lord sustained me and comforted me in ways I cannot put into words. It was not long until He reached out to me and let me know without doubt that I will be alright again.

It is this faith, hope and love that eventually put all the little drawers of my mind back into place. Many people go to a psychiatrist or councilor to find peace after a tragedy happens. While there is nothing wrong with having others to help, God is infinitely better and doesn't charge anything either. With His council come many other wonderful benefits like joy, peace, confidence and the sure knowledge that He loves me, no matter what. Most importantly, He doesn't expect me to do it all on my own, but I can rely on Him to help me and lean on Him when times get rough.

There are seven stages of grief that are common to everyone. These do not have to be experienced in this order, but are a guideline for you to understand, that what you are going through is the normal process of your mind sorting out your loss. It is not an orderly way, but a process that normally lasts between 1 to 2 years, sometimes longer. No one stage is more important than the other, but all are necessary for you to go through. Do not rush the process or deny any part of it, but let it happen naturally. Be patient and trust the Lord. He is right there with you. Deep wounds of the soul require more time to heal than the wounds of the body.

Shock - it is a form of protection to help you deal with what happened during the first few days.

Denial - it is the inability of the mind and heart to accept reality, because of the pain and anguish it would cause if you did.

Anger - it is the desire to strike out, punish or blame someone for what happened, including yourself and God.

Bargaining - it is the hope that you can somehow change the outcome if you will do better.

Depression - it is the realization that you can't change anything and so experience hopelessness and despair.

Acceptance - it is the stage where you know God has everything under control and His will is perfect in all things.

Reinvestment - it is the absence of pain and sorrow every time you think about the loss and a desire to love again without guilt.

"I will never leave you nor forsake you." Hebrew 13:5

Chapter 7

Fear of the Future

We think we are strong in faith when everything goes well – until it doesn't. It is surprising what part of our trust in God shows up lacking during a time of loss.

There is a quiet desperation in the area of finances, especially in women, after the death of their husband. I never thought much about money, because Allen took care of the bills. And then after he died, it somehow didn't seem fitting to talk about it until the proper time of mourning had passed.

It is strange, as Christians we think it is bad to concentrate on something as terrible as money, as if God doesn't understand we need it for daily living. And so, in the quiet, lonely hours of the evening, my financial situation came crushing in on me. Theoretically, I trusted the Lord, but realistically, there was not enough to pay the bills, since Allen's salary was now missing and mine not enough to cover everything. I didn't feel I could talk to Micah, since he was burdened enough about the loss of his father. Neither did I want to tell anyone else for fear of it being looked on as worldly and lacking trust in the Lord. That left me with only with my limited faith that God would provide.

I truly believe, if you want to know how much you trust the Lord, wait for those lonely hours at night, when no one is there to encourage you, help you or knows how you really feel in your heart. It is as if the walls of spiritual pretense is coming down and the real you appears from out of nowhere. Mind you, God already knows your heart and how little faith you actually have. The wonderful thing is, He loves you right where you are at that moment as you stand before Him like a little shorn sheep, looking pitiful and pathetic. If you have ever seen a freshly shorn sheep, you will know what I mean.

Gone was my luxurious coat of faith I thought I had; gone the trust in His provision and the certainty of His love I was so sure of before. They had fallen down in a heap, taken off by the shears of worry, anxiety and unbelief that God would understand and help me.

What would my friends say if they could see me now? It is this shame that causes us to withdraw and hide our fear of our financial future by having to admit how important money really is to us. It helps to admit to the Lord MONEY IS IMPORTANT and to believe He knows. It is the love of money God doesn't like or when we put it ahead of our love for Him.

I had to face my fears and worries when I found out the life insurance policy Allen had taken out just six months before, would not be paid out until it was determined that his death was not caused by a pre-existing condition. There was no telling how long the investigation would last, while my money to pay bills would run out real soon. My faith was dropping fast every time I looked at my bank account. Anger rose up in me against Allen for having left me in this mess, knowing full well it wasn't his fault. Every time I prayed, all I could think of was, there is no way God can get me out of this. No way!

A whole month went by and I decided I would really try real hard to get by one day at a time. Yet every time I thought the future, I would lose it and start crying. I tried to ignored the bills and put them in a drawer so I wouldn't have to look at them. Every now and then I would take out one or two that were almost overdo and pay them. After all, we have to have electricity and a phone. Next month I would have to turn the cable off and other things we could do without. I spent hours trying to decide how to get by without some of the things I had taken for granted. Who needs to get their nails done or buy new clothes? Surely I can go to a cheaper grocery store and buy stuff on sale? The more I mulled over these practical ways to save money, the more I realized nothing would help with the monthly bills that had to be paid and the worries took over my mind.

Maybe God didn't care or wasn't listening. Maybe I had done something wrong and offended Him and He was letting me stew a while. The whispers of the enemy in my ear were endless.

In spite of my lack of faith, worry and terrible anxiety, the Lord's answer came in a most unusual way. In July, I was talking to Barbara Lloyd, a friend from church one Sunday. Out of the blue she asked me about an insurance policy we had with the company she worked for.

"We did have it, but Allen dropped it years ago."

"Get me the information and I will check it out, Ethel," she said. "You never know, they may not have paid you out then."

"I don't think I have the policy papers any more, it's been so long ago."

"Just give me what you can remember or any paperwork you might have. I will try and see what I can do."

A few weeks later, at the precise time when I had reached a critical point in my financial situation, she called me and told me, according to God's calculations, I had $5000.00 in that account! I know the Lord was smiling when I thanked Him and then asked for forgiveness for my unbelief. He looked down on His little sheep like a loving Father, letting me know He would always take care of me, no matter my failings.

As I lay in bed that night I wondered, would I do better the next time when I hit a rough spot?

Well, I didn't.

As the months went by and I didn't hear from the Insurance company, my faith was dropping again as the worries returned and the bills piled up once more. What if they found a loophole and didn't pay? What if...? The list was endless as I lay there and played the worry game.

During this time, I had confided in my Mom and she became a source of strength and encouragement. At least I had learned one thing, I did not keep all this to myself. She helped me try to trust the Lord for just one day at a time like a child without thinking what might or might not happen. I was somewhat successful after she would pray for me daily and pointed out scripture verses about the faithfulness of God.

It was still scary and difficult and became worse as time went on. I noticed a pattern, when I was filled with trust in the Lord, the worries left me. When I was filled with worry, my trust vanished. You would think I would keep the trust and skip the worrying, since it didn't do anything but make matters worse. But it is easier said than done. My mind, with the enemy's help, played out scary scenarios like a loop in endless repetition until I believed them instead of what God says in His Word.

I wish I could have read the Bible each time the loop started, but it was somehow easier to listen to the gloomy predictions of what could happen. All the knowledge of God's love and goodness was washed away by this avalanche of negativity in my mind. In theory I realized none of it was true and a figment of my imagination, yet my mind had become the battle ground between faith and doubt over the love and faithfulness of God.

Every sin starts in the mind and can only be defeated in the mind. What I forgot at that time was I control my mind and I have the power to defeat the enemy, not by myself, but in the Name of Jesus. Could it have been that the Lord wanted to teach me, in order to make it in the future, I have to rely not just on His provisions, but on HIM and the power of His Name?

"Seek ye first the Kingdom of God and His righteousness, and all these things shall be added unto you. (Matthew 6:33)

After six months, once again, the money situation was at a critical point and I spent sleepless nights, crying, tossing and turning, filled with worry and anxiety about how to face the next day. The bills were piling up and I had no idea what to do. It was hard for me to face the fact that my faith was waning fast - again. What would my friends at church think of me if they knew? I once again gave in to doubt and the whispers of the enemy returned worse than before.

Why was God not doing anything to help me? Why is the insurance company not contacting me and letting me know what is going on? Even bad news would be better than no news at all. My faith was at the lowest point I had ever experienced and if it hadn't been for my Mom, I would have given up in despair. She was like a solid rock, unwavering in her assurance that the Lord would come to the rescue at exactly the right time. I hung on to her words like they were manna from heaven.

It was at this point, my church had a revival with a speaker from out of town. At first, I didn't want to go. What's the use to watch all those excited, happy people praising the Lord when I was scared, lonely and almost without hope about my situation.

I went at the urging of a friend in spite of being prepared to sit there in secret despair. *I need a word from You, Lord. Some sort of reassurance to let me know You care and will help me. PLEASE*! I was sitting in the pew, close to crying when I prayed this desperate prayer. Then suddenly, the Evangelist stood in front of me, took me by the hand and led me to the front of the church. I stood there, surprised, embarrassed and yet somehow hopeful. Maybe the Lord heard me?

"I have heard you," the man said, "I know you have been waiting for an answer for a long time. Take heart, the Lord would have you know He will take care of the problem. It is solved and good news is on the way." I don't remember all the words exactly, but I knew the Lord had spoken. For the first time in many days my heart was filled with hope and even joy. *Thank you, Lord, You are faithful and I will trust You. Please, forgive me my unbelief and doubt.*

That night I slept good for the first time in many nights. A few days later, a letter came from the insurance company. They were ready to pay out, all they needed was Allen's birth certificate! Thank You, Lord. There was only one thing wrong, I forgot where it was and spent hours looking for it. Just when I was ready to travel to Philadelphia to city hall, I remembered it was in the safe deposit box at the bank.

It had been six months by the time the check came. I realized I had not passed the 'money test' with flying colors. I knew the Lord never let me Micah go hungry in spite of it. This brought on understanding of the wonderful realization of being in His tender care no matter my failings.

That is what I love about God, He turned my unbelief into strong faith, not with anger but with His unconditional love. I now understand why I went through this time, because I needed to learn about His faithfulness and tender mercies He shows me every morning, like the Psalmist says. This time of testing also taught me we are always growing in Christ. There are times we wish we could be further along. To walk in faith and trust in Him is not something I knew how to do until He showed me how little I trusted Him when times get tough. I know today, without Him I am nothing and with Him, I can do all things, just like His Word says.

Learning to walk with the Lord is like going to school. Book knowledge is necessary, but without practical application, it remains theory. Many of us think reading the Bible is enough, but the Lord says in James 2:14 that our faith is dead if we don't act on what the Word of God says.

Obedience is really all God needs to accomplish what He wants to do with our life. He does not need our talents, money or anything else we have to offer. I can have all the faith in the world, if I don't trust Him and do what He tells me, it is useless. It takes faith as well as trust to be able to obey Him when we don't understand what He is doing with us and through us. Actually, I think the Lord has a formula for us and that is to accomplish His will in our lives as we walk with Him. If we love Him, these are necessary in order to please Him:

Faith + Trust = Obedience

Notice, none of these involve anything we can grasp with our hands, but only with our heart and mind. But if we chose to apply them, He is ready to pour out His grace, mercy and power over us beyond anything we could ever hope for.

"Trust in the Lord with all your heart and lean not on your own understanding. In all your ways acknowledge Him and He will direct your path." Proverbs 3-5

Chapter 8

The Road to Normal

T he transition from what was once normal to what it is now, was a difficult and long process. While memories are good, they can put roadblocks in the way of our recovery. Just when my heart was convinced I had made it without Allen, a special day or occasion would pop up on the calendar and I was thrown back to where I started in my journey of handling my grief.

It was a tradition to spend Thanksgiving with my in-laws in Germantown, Philadelphia. My mother-in-law would fix the turkey dinner with all the trimmings for the family. Allen's two brothers William and Ricky were already there when Micah and I arrived. It was good to see everyone. While Junior, as we called William, was a quiet man, his brother Ricky was a big, robust guy, who brought a different girlfriend every year. It was always amusing to see if Dorothy, my mother-in-law, would remember her name. In spite of everyone's best effort, she would invariably come up with the one from last year and it would cause an embarrassing moment for Ricky and the rest of us, to say nothing of his girlfriend.

Mom would mumble something about 'who can keep up with them' until she went even further back with the one from two years ago the next time. It became a standard joke in the family with all of us wondering who Ricky would bring this time.

Micah and I had a great time and the sorrow that Allen was missing among us, bound us together as a family that day. It felt good to share memories and incidents as we sat around the dinner table. We actually laughed at Allen's jokes and pranks he loved to pull on everyone. It turned out to be a good day and it was wonderful to see Micah laugh. It had been a long time.

Another such day came all too soon. It was December 3rd and it was supposed to be our 20th wedding anniversary. When I woke up, the weather was as downcast as my mind. I had dreaded the day since Allen passed away, knowing I would be in a terrible state. Every one of the emotions I thought I had so well under control came crushing in on me that morning the moment I looked over where he used to lie in bed next to me.

Instead of having a great time on that cruise he promised me, I was alone at home with my thoughts of anger, hurt and pain. Anger against Allen for leaving me, anger against God for taking him and pain because I couldn't do anything to overcome the loneliness that descended on me like a heavy weight on my chest. It is this feeling of being left behind and facing the future without him that overwhelmed me that morning. How could I possibly deal with the endless, bleak days of sorrow and isolation which stretched ahead of me? It seemed like a long road with no light at the end of the tunnel. Life suddenly looked dreary and without hope without Allen; and at that moment, I was convinced it would always be that way.

It was hard to trust the Lord, to see His love or feel His presence as grief overwhelmed me and drowned out my faith. I felt alone, helpless and abandoned. *Why doesn't anyone care or see how much I hurt? God, why don't You care? This is all so unfair.*

It felt as if I was thrown back to the moment I found out Allen had died. All the progress I thought I had made was gone and I was devastated. Had I really tried all these months for nothing?

During the day I held my thoughts together for Micah, but they came rushing back as soon as I was alone in bed. I literally wallowed in a heart-wrenching pity party and cried until my pillow was soaked with tears. I couldn't and didn't want to stop until I was totally exhausted and lay there as if waiting for God to come and comfort me. And He did. In the stillness, His gentle Spirit filled my heart. As I turned to Him, my faith and trust returned and I felt His peace envelop me until I fell into a sweet, restful sleep.

"When you lie down you will not be afraid; yes, you will lie down and your sleep will be sweet." Proverbs 3:24

Grieving is not an orderly process, but a time when holidays, sudden memories or anything else can trigger a strong reaction of intense loss. And then there are times when it happens for no reason at all.

GRIEVING IS NOT A SIGN OF LACK OF FAITH, but a necessary process. These sudden bouts of loneliness, despair, anger, weeping or any other strong emotions are normal and actually help us in the long run to deal with our loss. It is as if they need to surface every now and then so we can deal with them and wash them away with our tears. It is perfectly normal to have faith and trust in the Lord one day and wallow helplessly in negative emotions the next. God understands and like He did that night, He gives us peace like only He can give. The Lord does not always change our circumstances, but wants to change us, so we can learn to deal with our problems better by putting them in His hands instead of trying to manage them on our own.

It is good to be in that place when we stop fretting, realizing it doesn't do anything but make us feel worse. The Father wants us to believe what Jesus told us,

"Peace I leave with you; my peace I give you. I do not give to you as the world gives. Do not let your hearts be troubled and do not be afraid." John 14:27

However, there is a difference between fretting and allowing grief to run its course. Grieving is not lack of faith and trust, but releasing and sorting out feelings that need to be felt in order for us to heal.

Fretting is another word for worrying. And worrying is doubting that God cannot or will not handle things at the present, like finances or anything else in our life. When we give in to such feelings, the enemy comes in like a flood with those negative, hopeless and gloomy thoughts that God doesn't care and all is lost. That is the time we need to read His Word, turn to a friend or family member or attend a grief group.

What is the difference then between real grief and worrying? Real grief deals with our emotions about the loss of a loved one, worrying deals with lack of trust in God's ability to provide for our daily bread. This does not just mean food, but finances and things we need, but His spiritual help as well. Worrying comes from the enemy, real grief comes from God and works like a soothing salve on our wounds of loss. That is the time He wants to hold us in His arms and comfort us with His Word.

If you don't know the Bible as well as you should, go to the internet and look for scriptures that address loss, grief and sorrow. When you find them, run them off and keep them close by so you can quote them out loud when the enemy comes whispering his lies in your ears. He cannot stand against the Word of God, but will flee if you stand against him with God's reassuring promises. This works especially well when you don't feel your faith, but want to give in to hopelessness, worry and fear.

Special days and holidays hold a strong meaning with certain traditions and wonderful memories for me. I measure the years not by numbers alone, but by what happened on any of these holidays.

Christmas is definitely one of the biggest memory builders. In our family, Allen's parents would come to our house to enjoy Micah opening up his toys. It started when Micah was little and we didn't want to take him outside in the cold weather. And so we invited everyone here since my in-laws only lived fifteen minutes away. Every year since then I would fix Christmas dinner at my house and we exchanged gifts with each other. Except this year. I did not feel like cooking. Micah and I decided together, we didn't want a tree or any decorations either. Instead, we put one candle in the picture window of the living room and felt it was enough. I took everybody out to a restaurant for dinner and then we all came back to the house for desert and opening gifts. It was a quiet occasion. We missed Allen's cheerful presence terribly. Micah was very quiet. It was definitely not anything like the other years and I was sort of glad when it was over. *Would any Christmas ever be like it had been,* I wondered later as I lay in bed.

I was glad to spend New Year's Eve in church. It was our tradition to be among my Christian brothers and sisters. It helped me not to feel alone as we asked the Lord's blessings for the next year. It felt wonderfully reassuring to go to the altar and pray as a church family. As we prayed, I knew things would get better and the Lord would be there to help me and Micah in the coming year.

It was the year 1989. Allen died six months ago and to my surprise, life had a way of going on as usual. But I was not the same and neither was Micah. A loss like we had experienced brought with it changes that not only affected our outward circumstances, but more so the inner make-up of our soul. It had wrought a new maturity and appreciation of what is really important in life in both of us.

I noticed I did not smile much anymore and the things I used to think of as funny, suddenly weren't. I am sure my co-workers and friends noticed the lack of my normal sense of humor. They tried to help, but were at a loss to know how. My friend Alice, the pastor's sister, also a widow, was a tremendous help to me during this time. She understood how I felt many times, even before I shared. The church Mother, Virginia Caswell, shared many words of wisdom with me which helped me cope and understand that life continues and I must trust and wait on the Lord. One of her favorite verses she shared with me was,

"I will lift up my eyes to the hills from whence comes my help. My help comes from the Lord who made heaven and earth." Psalm 121:1

I was entering the stage of learning to live with my loss. I realized I would never be the same. However, I also knew it did not mean that was necessarily bad. Everyone changes after their life is totally altered, their circumstances changed and the person they loved more than life, is gone forever. Adjusting to that loss is a necessary step to healing. It means I gained perspective on what happened by realizing that Allen was gone and I had to go on without him. It showed the initial feelings of acute loss I now experienced during difficult episodes brought on by certain memories and special days, was also normal.

This time brought on a feeling of wanting to feel secure in my friendship with family and friends and I had a strong fear of not wanting to lose anyone else. One of the ways it showed was that I became overprotective of Micah and worried constantly about him. Needless to say, he did not like it, but the mere thought of losing him would cause such feelings of abandonment, it took my breath away.

To this day, I thank my family and friends for sticking close to me and helping me get through this difficult period. Their visits, friendship and daily, little kindnesses did more than any counseling or medicine could have ever accomplished. How good it was to be loved not just by God, but by others as well.

"I will not die but live, and will proclaim what the Lord has done." Psalm 118:17

Chapter 9

Shared Grief

Everyone handles grief differently. There are no guidelines or a certain order in which it should be done, just so long we do not suppress it or try to rush it for one reason or another.

One area during this time caused me a great deal of trouble. I was overly concerned about Micah. Except for the day when I told him his father was dead, I never saw him cry. He seemed to have a strong desire to take care of me and be the man of the house, but never opened up to me in the early days. Instead, he stayed in his room. Every now and then I heard him cry, but when I asked if he wanted to talk, he just walked away with a sad smile,

"I'm ok, Mom."

But I knew he wasn't ok. It broke my heart to see him so sad and I was glad he had his friend Frankie to talk to. He is the one who lost his father two days before Allen died and I knew he was a great help to Micah in dealing with his feelings. Although I had no idea what they talked about.

One way I knew Micah was having a hard time was, he started talking back and acting out at times in a way he had never done before. I felt it was more than just being a teenager, but the struggle of trying to deal with the harsh reality of his father's death. The fact that he tried to take Allen's place in some areas, made it difficult for both of us and I had to remind him that he was not the parent, I was. I am sure he viewed himself a failure when he did not know how to be an adult at times when he thought he should be. Being a teenager under normal circumstances is tough enough, but trying to act grown up in the aftermath of such loss, was more than he could handle. Pushing himself into this role proved to be extremely difficult, not just for him, but also for me. This struggle led to some intense arguments and hurt feelings for both of us.

I cannot say that I was always the best I could have been with my overprotective attitude towards him. Looking back, it seems that while Micah tried so hard to be an adult, I wanted him to remain a child at all cost so I could keep him out of harm's way. Needless to say, this did not work very well at times and I wish I had understood the dynamics then as I do now. But this was our way of dealing with our grief during these difficult days. Our conflict was not that we did not love each other, but that we tried to protect one another to avoid any further loss.

Our feelings and reactions were driven by the fear of losing the only remaining person in our lives we knew neither one of us could do without. This caused a deep sense of anxiety and we both made many mistakes because of it.

Instead of talking about these feelings, we tried to protect the other and in the process started arguing instead of confiding in each other. Micah tried to take charge of situations he was not mature enough to handle and attempted to tell me what to do, while I asserted my place as a parent and demanded he obey me as his mother.

"I love you Micah and thank you for what you are trying to do for me, but I am still the parent and your mom and will take care of you." I reached out to him and hugged him and added, "Son, we will get through this together with God's help, prayer and sharing with each other."

He walked away that day with a sad little smile and said, "It's ok, Mom."

Through my friend Alice's grandson Biron, Micah found a job at UPS. It helped him take his mind off of Allen's death and our tension at home. The company paid both of them a bonus if they came in first in their assignments. Many days he would come home with a bright smile on his face,

"We beat them up again."

I was proud of him and told him so. I could see that he had decided to make a life for himself as time went on and it was good.

It was I who could not let go and worried constantly that he was getting in with the wrong crowd or get involved with a girl. So when he told me he invited a group of kids over one evening, including girls, I strongly objected and refused to allow them to come inside in no uncertain words, citing the late hour. It must have been very embarrassing for him to go back out and tell his friends his mother would not allow them to come in.

Looking back, I wish I had not done that, because my behavior did nothing to help him have a normal time with his peers. I should have been grateful he wanted them to come to our house, instead of hanging around somewhere else where I did not know what he was doing.

It is hard to look back and see all the wrong things we do when our mind is filled with fear and insecurity because of loss. It makes us want to control those around us and keep them close at all cost, because we don't want to lose them, too.

One of the hardest things, next to the loss of his father, was that Micah's dream of going to Virginia State University was shattered. I realized he could not confide his true feelings to me, but I could only imagine his anger, hurt and abandonment by his father at a time like this. How guilty he must have felt for feeling this way about his Dad. How abandoned and frustrated he felt having to give up his dream, because going to Virginia State with his good buddy and classmate Danny Curberson was all he wanted for a long time.

Micah had a hard time concentrating on school during these last months before graduation. Since he could not go to the college he wanted, it didn't seem all that important any longer and his grades began to suffer. This worried me since I wanted him to get a college education and do well and find a good job like any good mother.

In the end, Micah hung in there and graduated, because, more than anything, he wanted to honor his dad and have him be proud of him.

In April was the senior prom. It was a time of celebration and it helped pull him out of his shell and act like a teen. He was elated when he received a partial scholarship to Liberty Univerity, several awards in basked ball and soccer and Letters for good sportsmanship.

He took Greer, a lovely girl and special friend from church to the prom. She wore a hot pink dress and looked perfectly gorgeous. Micah got a cummerbund to match it, as well as hot pink socks to top it off. He looked like a real gentleman when he came down the stairs until he kicked up his legs, showing his socks off with a big smile. He had bought her a white corsage with his own money and looked really happy when he got into my Volvo to drive to her house to pick her up. I watched him take off, thinking that his dad would have been real proud of him. I felt terribly lonely as I followed the car down the road with my eyes filling up with tears. *Why couldn't Allen be here to share this?*

Later that evening, family, friends and church members came for a catered dinner at my home catered by my friend Vicky. It was a joyous time of fellowship and I had the feeling of a new beginning for Micah on his road to a new life.

Thank you, Lord for helping him find a healthy balance in his life between what was and what lies ahead, living life one day at a time and finding a new normal without his father.

Micah started Temple University in September 1989. He was a little overwhelmed in the beginning, but soon found his bearings. I was led by the Spirit to set up a special table for prayer in the living room. This is where Micah and I prayed together each morning before we both left the house for the day. It helped us take the next step toward healing and overcoming our grief. It was also a wonderful way to voice our feelings and concerns to God and so help us to understand each other better at the same time. Our relationship improved greatly as we learned about our worries, concerns and problems without having to talk about them, because we shared them with the Lord in our prayers. Thank You Lord for Your love and saving grace!

I also had come out of the initial stages of grief and found myself able to seek the Lord in a new and deeper way. Coming through tragedy brings maturity and maturity brings the wisdom to trust in the Lord. And this in turn brings inner healing. This was the time when I realized that I could go on without Allen and without falling apart or living in the past. I had faced my grief and acknowledged my hurt in many different ways and had come through it a stronger, better person. I realized God had been there all the time and would continue to sustain me in the future, no matter what. I am glad today I did not know what the future held or I would not have been so sure. Right then, I was certain I could face my life with faith, trust and love in the Lord and the certainty He would always be there for me.

There were still moments I broke down and cried at unexpected times, but I knew I would be alright. I had my work, my wonderful son and my family and friends. Life was starting to get back to normal. I felt I had come through the valley of the shadow of death and come out a stronger person on the other side.

It was a good feeling to realize I would and could make it, life would go on and the future was something I could finally face with a sense of hope. At the same time, I was able to remember Allen and our life together not just with grief, but with a sense of gratitude for the time we had together. I realized it was alright to talk about him with my friends and recall some of the things he did without crying.

Refusing to share about a loved one when talking to others, does nothing to help us overcome our grief or deal with their absence. It is silly to think I could possibly ignore the twenty years we had together by never talking about Allen. This would definitely not help me start a new life without him.

I remember the day when I realized, it is ok to smile or even laugh again without feeling guilty or being afraid people will think I had forgotten about Allen. I strongly felt, if he was here he would not want me to go through life sad from now on, remembering what a wonderfully cheerful person he had been. It was his positive attitude, his bright smile and boundless energy I had loved about him and the way he had made me smile with his silly antics. I knew without a doubt, he would not want to be around me crying and sad all the time. Remembering him in this positive way, helped me to be positive as well.

Micah and I had made it through the first year with its holidays and special occasions. Together, we celebrated his graduation and entry into college and it seemed the worst was over and we could both look into a hopeful future, knowing Allen would be pleased. We had both made mistakes, but even if Allen was still here, it didn't mean we would have been perfect all the time.

We both had our wonderful memories and shared the strong bond of love for him. That would never change. But we had changed and had become stronger and more sure that no matter what life deals us, the Lord will always be there.

"But to each of us grace has been given as Christ apportioned it."
Ephesians 3:7

Chapter 10

When God has other Plans

𝕴 t is a strange thing, just when we think we have learned to trust God in whatever life brings, something happens that shows us we are not quite there yet. There are many different aspects of trust. Some areas we go through have taught us, He will always be there, until we enter a new phase or realm in our life that is not familiar and then, we need to learn to rely on Him all over again.

Walking and growing in the Lord is like climbing a ladder. Just when we have finished one rung and think we have it down pat, He pushes us up to the next. While we felt secure and sure of ourselves of having learned the lesson of the previous one, we know nothing about what we need to learn on the next and so have to start from the beginning. It is called gaining maturity one day at a time in the specific areas, He wants us to learn in our walk with Him. It is an ongoing process that never stops until we reach the top of the ladder on the day of our home going.

This principle was brought home to me in a way I would have never expected. Both Micah and I had settled into a routine of daily life, feeling the heavy load of sadness had lifted and we had made a fresh start. I was back at work and he was attending college. It felt like a new beginning for us, a fresh start in a world that was no longer this dark and scary, lonely place.

I had made plans to attend a church conference in Birmingham and was looking forward to visiting my family while I was there.

I had shared at church not long ago now that I had been knocked down by Allen's death, but not knocked out.

"The devil will just have to try something else, for I trust God and will not turn from Him, no matter what," I had shared with conviction.

It is never good to challenge the enemy, but rather it is better to trust the Lord. While I had learned to handle the first stage of grief on the first rung of the ladder, I had no idea how to do as well on the second. The Lord must have smiled at my confidence. Thank goodness, like a loving Father, He knew I had a long way to go to reach the top and loved me just the same.

It was a regular morning. Micah was still asleep when I walked out the front door to my car. There were patches of snow on the ground. Just as I opened the door, I realized I had forgotten my lunch and walked back inside to get it. That is when it happened, my boots must have still been wet in spite of me wiping them off carefully. I slipped and fell just as I reached the kitchen. I heard the bones crack as I landed on my left ankle with my full weight. For some reason, amidst the searing pain, I wondered what this would do to my trip to Birmingham.

Micah came rushing down the steps and immediately reached for the phone to call 911.

"Where are you hurt, Mom?"

"It's my ankle. You've got to take my shoes off, Baby. They are my brand new black suede boots and I don't want the EMT's to cut them," I managed to say between clenched teeth as I lay on the floor in terrible pain.

"You're worried about your boots?"

"Just do it."

"It's going to hurt, Mom."

"I know it will, but I really want to keep these boots." I had no idea why this was so important to me, but Micah managed to unzip the boot and gently slid it off my already swollen ankle. It hurt terribly and I groaned in pain. When I looked at my foot, I saw it was dangling at a strange angle.

I was taken to the hospital and after several tests, the doctor decided that it was a difficult, compound fracture of my left ankle. He ordered my immediate transport to another facility, where there was a well-known orthopedic specialist. In his words, there was a good chance I might never walk again.

The surgeon had to put three screws on one side of my ankle and a metal plate and a pin on the other. Not only that, a big, heavy cast covered my leg from the thigh to my foot, which left me unable to move much, least of all walk. I was told I had to stay in bed for four to six weeks with the exception of using the facilities, with no shower or any other movement. I was released from the hospital after two days with instructions to come back in four weeks to have the cast checked.

I had time to think and worry while I was in the hospital. With Allen gone, who would take care of me? Micah had his school plus a part time job. Besides, how could a nineteen-year old boy be expected to tend to his mother? I couldn't take a shower, there were sheets to be changed and meals to fix. The list got longer the more I thought about it. Fear and anxiety washed over me like a flood and drowned out the constant pain.

Talking to my mother, I realized she could not come and help me since my Dad was very ill. I felt panic and fear when I hung up. There was no one but Micah, since my brothers and sisters were working and busy with their own lives. I wondered what God was doing and why He had allowed this to happen. It made no sense, just like Allen's death made no sense.

Life had just gotten back to somewhat normal, Lord and now this. I don't understand Your ways. Why? What am I going to do lying in bed for weeks, totally dependent on my young son to take care of me. It is too much for him; he is too young to handle that kind of responsibility for that length of time.

What are You trying to teach me? What is it I can learn laying in this bed for so long? I want to go to work and help Micah instead of him helping me. I don't want to ask my friends and neighbors; they will get tired of helping me after all they did since Allen died. Please, Lord, tell me what to do?

It was quite a feat to get upstairs when I got home. My bedroom would be my home for many weeks. I had Micah bring everything I might need up to me, like my computer, books and everything else I could think of. He was so very helpful and even cheerful and seemed pleased that he could finally be in charge. I cringed at the thought of now had to trust him to do everything I thought he was not able to do before. He had told me so many times he would take care of me after Allen's death, and now he really had his chance.

"Are you sure you can handle this, Micah?" I asked him after I settled in. "I am afraid this may be too much for you, Baby."

"I am going to give it a try, Mom." He leaned over and hugged me. "I got this, don't worry."

All my worries and fears that I would languish alone for those many weeks, were a lie of the enemy. Micah fixed breakfast every morning and we had our daily devotion before he headed off to school.

Once again, my neighbors, church family and many others, took turns visiting me almost every day and came with encouragement, cheer and hope plus food.

The ladies in my neighborhood on Rodney Street and Linwood Road, as well as friends from the church, came to the rescue and supplied us with food for lunch and dinner almost every day. I am still amazed at the faithfulness and love they showed me during this time. It became quite a ritual for me to throw the key out of my window down to the front door each time someone came to visit. Thank goodness, my bed was close enough for me to toss it out to them from upstairs. It's amazing how the Lord thinks of all these little things!

My Mom called every day with a word and prayer. The Pastor made frequent visits as well and after a while, I realized how much everyone loved me. It is one thing for church friends to say 'I love you', it is another when they prove it through practical things like food, visits and prayer.

One lady from the church named Earline, a godly, quiet woman, came one day to visit. She told me the Lord instructed her to clean my house once a week. She was not very educated or prominent in the church, but down to earth, practical and a hard worker. My house had never been that clean on my best days when she got through with it, since I am not one for perfect order. Every week she came for the many months I was laid up in bed. She took no money for it and looked on it as an assignment from the Lord.

This act of kindness ministered to me more than anything and I was humbled by her faith and obedience to the Lord. Many of us want to have great ministries and lead thousands to the Lord, but I saw in Earline a giant in the faith. In the scheme of things, what she did was not much, but in God's eyes, He must have been pleased by her service. There are many mansions in heaven that will be occupied by saints like her, while the smaller places will have some surprised people in them, given their prominence and stature in the church. I wondered if I would be as faithful as this simple woman and what size my mansion will be.

When someone asked one day what it is that determines the size of our place in heaven, the Lord showed them a simple math. Every time we obey Him and do cheerfully what He has for us to do, a brick is sent up. In the end, *we* decide how big our dwelling place will be, not God. He just uses what we send up.

There comes a time, when grief gives way to a time when we can accept what has happened and life seems to get back to normal. During this stage, there can be a lot of guilt at enjoying the normal, because we think we are in danger of forgetting our loved one. Just as no one can be happy all the time, no one can be sad continuously either. Daily life has a way of lessening our feelings of sadness and grief; and that is good.

There will always be times when we feel our sorrow intensely, but to think that we have to feel this way all the time to prove our love, is not what true grief is all about. During this time, there needs to be a mixture of sadness and happy memories, of sorrow and the first signs of hope that we can go on with life in a normal way without the loved one we lost.

For as much as I still grieved for Allen, my present situation of being trapped in the bed took over. Unable to do anything for myself, go to work or church or be productive in any way, it took most of my thoughts. Where there was grief before, now there was frustration. Where there was sadness for losing Allen, now there was anger for being unable to do anything I wanted to do other than stare at these four walls.

My grief this time was not about Allen, but about me those first few weeks. It wasn't so much grief, but frustration and anger how this could have happened just when everything was getting better. I had a lot of questions for God, but He did not answer any of them. Looking back, it was more like me throwing a temper tantrum while He looked on with a smile, knowing I would eventually get over it.

To grieve does not make life stop, but it is a way to help us go on. Part of this process is that our life and its challenges continue and we are able to deal with the problems of every-day living.

"Submit yourselves, then to God. Resist the devil and he will flee from you. Come near to God and he will come near to you."
James 3:7-8

Chapter 11

Be still and know that I am God

In the weeks that followed, which seemed like forced confinement and frustration at first, turned into a time of finding peace and spiritual growth. I learned to read the Bible without hurrying and had many wonderful conversations with God.

Each day started with Micah and I praying together. With his new responsibility of caring for me, I watched him grow into a man of God. He trusted me more and opened up as we talked about finances and other daily problems that needed to be handled. Both of us felt our relationship was improving in spite of my circumstances. I was proud of him the way he handled everything, while he felt good that he could finally be 'the man of the house', the way he wanted. While he never really talked about Allen's death, I could tell, he was dealing with it much better. In the days, weeks and months following my fall, Micah and I began to understand each other in the area of our feelings and emotions. We realized, each of us had found a way to grieve and heal in our own way and it was good. We both knew we were going to make it and build a new life with the Lord's help.

In my prayers I was still asking God, what He was trying to teach me through all this, but He never answered. Let's face it, sliding down the stairs on my behind when it was time to go to the doctor to have my cast checked, did not fit in with any lessons I thought I needed to learn. Taking sponge baths was getting old and I finally figured out how to wrap my leg in a big towel, hang it out over the bathtub and sit on a chair while the water runs over me. It is amazing how such little things like a shower get to mean so much when we are forced to do without.

My relationship with the Lord grew and I learned to trust Him. What choice did I have, since I couldn't see a reason for any of this? I became much more aware of His presence as time went on and learned to look to Him for everything.

I never understood the verse in Psalm 23 where the Shepherd makes the sheep to lie down in green pastures until I was there. It was the only place where I could think of His goodness and mercy and realize fully how He had brought Micah and me through all this so far. His provision, grace and mercy became clear to me and I began to line up the many ways He had taken care of us.

First of all, I had my family and the many friends who stood by us for these past months. Then the Lord made sure our finances were taken care of even now, since I had signed up for disability insurance when I started working at the University. Another blessing was that Micah's college was free. I was particularly touched how the Lord even sent someone to clean the house for me. He had thought of everything and I was so grateful, it brought tears to my eyes. He had made me be still and know that He is God by allowing me to lie in the bed, able to take time to grow and draw closer to Him through prayer.

It was when I quit struggling, He gave me songs in the night that lifted my faith to a higher level. It was not surprising, each had to do with trusting Him!

One day, a lady from church named Lerotha Hunter came and sang the simple song, 'Yes, Jesus Loves Me'. I had heard the song since I was a child, but as she sang it with her clear, operatic voice, the melody and childlike words touched my soul. It was as if God had sent an angel to minister to me and it made me feel grateful.

It is still amazing to this day, how God touched me in so many wonderful ways as I was still before Him. I was healing not just in my leg, but in my spirit during this time. I spent many hours reading His Word and it brought life into my heart and soul. I would have never been able to have this kind of close fellowship with Him had I not been made to lie down in my room for so many weeks. During this time, I went from struggling to accepting my circumstances and in return received His love and encouragement in ways I had never experienced before. He showed me His love by teaching me to be grateful for His provision and the tender care He poured out on me.

Gratitude is the perfect antidote to despair, depression and sorrow. It is so much more profitable to remember the faithfulness of God in the past than concentrate on the uncertainties of the future. Remembering God's goodness brings praise, joy and hope, while fear of the days ahead fills us with anxiety, frustration and hopelessness. We make the choice which way we want to follow.

It is sad that the Lord had to make me to lie down in the green pastures of His Word for me to come to this point of trust, hope and joy in Him. But how grateful I am He did, because I would look at this time with a thankful heart in the difficult days ahead. It prepared me in ways I could have never managed on my own if I had been busy with work, church and everyday living. No wonder He did not answer my constant question of "Why is this happening?"

And this is the depth of His love for us, that He allows us to throw our little temper tantrums without being influenced to change our circumstances, because He knows we will need what it is we are supposed to learn during this time. There is no uncertainty with God, neither is He surprised by anything. Like a loving father, He does not look at what we are, but what we can be and will become under His masterful hands. Change is painful, confusing and scary, but it is necessary to go through and accept if we want to become what God has purposed for us.

"For we are his workmanship, created in Christ Jesus to do good works, which God prepared in advance for us to do." Ephesians 2:10

I look at this incident as a foreshadowing of what was to come. My broken ankle represents my broken life after Allen's death. By trusting in the Lord and drawing close to Him, taking time to read His Word and holding still under His care, He had a chance to not just heal my bones, but my soul as well.

In ancient days, when the shepherd had a sheep that would not stay close to the flock, but run off repeatedly and have to be rescued constantly from its own disobedience, the shepherd had no choice but to break its legs. Because if he didn't, the little sheep would get killed by wild animals as it roamed outside of the shepherd's protection. This way, it was forced to lie down until it was healed. During that time, he did not abandon it, but would carry it on his shoulders and put it down gently in the lush pasture, so that it could still feed and stay close to him.

I am not saying that the Lord broke my ankle, but He used this time to make me to lie down and listen to His voice and help me to stay in His presence. It was then, I learned to listen and hear His quiet, still voice as He prepared me for the tragic days to come. When they did, I would hold still so He could carry me on His shoulders and to make sure I would be close to Him.

When a wound heals, the place where the scar forms, is stronger than the rest of the skin. During this time with the Lord, He allowed my scars from Allen's death to heal and form a strong faith in His love in the area of dealing with my loss. How grateful I am to this day for my confinement during this time. I don't think I could have ever gotten through without it in the days to come.

After several cast changes and five months later, the day finally arrived when they took off the cast and I could walk again with the aid of crutches. I still had to go to physical therapy, but by the time May came, I was able to go back to work.

I am sure Micah was glad to have his time as caregiver come to an end. He had also healed and was smiling again like he used to. I was happy for him, because he was getting closer to Greer, the girl he had taken to the prom. She was lovely, beautiful inside and out and a good Christian.

I had taken my place back as the parent in our relationship and that brought some tense moments just like it did before. But both of us had learned to tolerate and understand our feelings much more than before. I just hoped Micah would wait until his education was finished before seriously getting involved. He was changing from Temple Ambler to the main campus and was excited, because some of his friends were there. It was wonderful that he was a regular, happy young man, spending time with friends while going to school.

I was eager to go back to work as well, although still on crutches and going to physical therapy. The 'normal' I had so longed for before, was finally here. Micah and I would be alright and while we both still talked a lot about Allen, it didn't hurt so much anymore, but brought out many happy memories. It is wonderful how our mind only remembers the good things, while the bad fade away after a while. We both knew our love for Allen would always be there and keep the bond between us strong, no matter what.

The grieving process had taken its course and we both had arrived at the place of acceptance and ready to reach out to love again. That doesn't mean I looked for male companionship, but Micah had found someone he could love in Greer. I was content with my memories and not interested in finding anyone to replace Allen. At the same time, I was not lonely with my family close by and my church family and the ladies in my neighborhood. All of them had certainly proven their love during these many months by standing by us during our time of trouble.

Because I had just gone back to work, Micah and I couldn't go to Alabama for the big family reunion during the 4th of July. Instead, the neighborhood decided to have a large block party. It was a lot of fun and I got to see the countless people who had been so faithful to us and thank them for their love. The day was a big success with fire crackers, good food and fellowship. Life was good again.

Soon it was time for school to start and Pastor Morris had asked the church to take some time in the morning to pray for the children. On this particular morning, the Lord urged me to go, crutches and all, and join in prayer with many others for Micah, his change on campus and that he stay the course with his studies.

The next morning, Micah and I prayed together as usual. I hugged him and kissed him afterwards and just as usual, he pretended to be annoyed when I got emotional. After all, he was nineteen by now!

As I was walking out the door, he ran back upstairs to get ready. He was excited to pick up his paycheck at work today.

"Don't forget, it's trash day!" I shouted after him.

"Don't worry, Mom, I got this," he answered with his favorite phrase.

My gaze followed him up the stairs, and I suddenly felt like praying.

"God, do whatever You have to do to keep Micah in Your care and allow him to get to know You the way I do." I was a little afraid what God might have to do in order to answer that prayer and so I added, "Please, Lord, help me to stand."

Later at church, I prayed the whole hour for Micah and the other children going back to school. I went on to work with a happy heart because Micah was in the Lord's hands. What could possibly happen to him?

"And we know that in all things God works for the good of those who love him, who have been called according to his purpose." Romans 8:28

Chapter 12

A Road twice traveled

$\mathfrak{I}$t was a day like every other day. I was at work when the call came from Einstein Hospital.

"Mrs. Perkins, your son has been in a car accident. Please come to the Hospital immediately."

My co-worker Gilda offered to come with me for the fifteen-minute drive.

"I hope he is not hurt too bad, I would hate for his car insurance to go up," I told her on the way.

"He is a good driver, I'm sure they will give him some slack." She sounded confident. "Everything is going to be alright."

We rushed through the emergency room entrance and asked for Micah. The guard asked if we were here for the two young men who had just been brought in.

"No, I'm looking for my son, he was in a car accident," I answered.

"Just go down the hall to the desk and a nurse will take you to his room," he said with a slight hesitation in his voice.

A nurse seemed to be waiting for us.

"Please, follow me and I will take you there." She did not answer when I asked her how Micah was.

This is not right, I thought when we entered a room with a table and chairs around it. *This is not a patient room.*

"The doctor will be right with you," she said and left.

"I do not feel good about this, Gilda," I said as I felt the beginning of pain in my stomach and a feeling of dread washed over me.

After a short while, the doctor came in. He looked at us with a solemn expression and asked,

"Which one of you is Mrs. Perkins?"

"I am."

"Please, sit down, Mrs. Perkins." He pointed to a chair at the table. I suddenly realized I was still standing with my crutches and my leg was starting to hurt.

"We did all we could, Ma'am, I am so sorry for your loss."

I stared at him, trying to comprehend. My mind was reeling.

"You cannot tell me that!" I finally said with rising panic in my voice. "There is no way you can tell me bad news. Look at me, I am on crutches and I just lost my husband two years ago." I was shouting by now. "Can't you see I can't take this kind of bad news? Please!"

"I am so sorry, Mrs. Perkins. Your son's body was so mangled, when we got the bleeding under control in one area, another would start, until there were too many. We just could not save him."

I stared at him, numb and in shock and his voice sounded far away when he said,

"I will take you to him, come, follow me to the room next door."

In a daze I looked at Micah. He was covered with a sheet from the neck down. His head was bandaged and he had a big bruise on his left cheek. I stared at his face and realized, my wonderful, sweet boy, my only child was DEAD!

I cried softly as I asked God to help me. And then, out of the depth of my being, an unbearable pain overwhelmed me and I let out a piercing scream.

"Lord, You took my only child. He was all I had left!" And then I stood in silence, staring at Micah's face, unable to think, speak or move. Suddenly, into the stillness, the presence of God came like a big embrace and I heard His voice, I WILL NOT LEAVE YOU NOR FORSAKE YOU.

It was so real, I looked around to see if anyone else had heard it. Instead, the Doctor asked me if I wanted a shot to help me calm down. I looked at Gilda. She was crying.

"No, thank you, I will be alright," I answered and started crying again.

"Do you want us to call your family?" the Doctor asked gently. I can ask the nurse to do that right away."

"Yes, please."

The nurse called my brother John in New Jersey and my pastor, Bishop Ernest Morris.

Since I didn't want my in-laws to hear about this on the news, I decided to drive to their home in Germantown. I knew they never missed watching it.

I walked up to their door with a feeling of dread.

My mother-in-law was inconsolable and screamed 'No, no, no!' when I told them and repeated the name of Micah over and over again. My father-in-law sat in his chair, crying softly. After a while, Junior, Allen's brother, came and I had to tell him what happened. It was terrible to watch his face as he went into shock. After a while, he walked over to me and managed to say,

"I am so sorry, Ethel."

After that we sat and cried.

I have no idea how I got home, but somehow I made it. I know the Lord was with me and protected me on the road.

Not long after, the house was filled with friends, people from the church, neighbors and co-workers. When my brother John came, he hugged me and asked what he could do. I told him to call our parents and the family in Alabama. Everything was like in a daze around me.

"Tell Mom I will talk to her later. I need a little time right now and will call her as soon as possible." I wanted to calm down some so I could help her deal with the news.

My sister Jean had just moved back to Alabama last week. I missed her. When I finally called my mother, it was she who reassured me and I was glad to hear her strong faith and her love for me.

Bishop Morris and his wife Winifred, as well as the Youth Minister, Elder Chaver, and some of the other ministers of the church, came and prayed for me. I took great comfort in that. They assured me they would send someone tomorrow to help with the arrangements.

My friend Keasley once again stood by me with the practical things like organizing everything for the home going. Together with my friend Carol, they took charge and saw to it, people left when it was time for me to get some rest for the night. Keasley spent the night and it felt comforting not to be alone.

But that night I experienced a nightmare, except I had my eyes open. Sleep would not come and I tossed and turned while crying. While the pain was not physical, it hurt just as much and I was in such agony that I was hoping I would not have to wake up. Each time I thought about Micah, it was as if knives were cutting into my belly and my heart and I would double over and start sobbing. It was the most endless night I have ever spent in my life.

As I was crying out WHY GOD, WHY, I reached over to turn the radio on. It was set on a Gospel station and played the song, GOD IS GOD – AND HE CAN DO WHATEVER HE WANTS TO – WHENEVER HE WANTS TO – AND HOWEVER HE WANTS TO. *For real, God, that is Your answer to me?* I lay and listened and then cried even harder. *This is not the New Year or the new life I was looking for. Everyone in my family is gone. First Allen and now Micah. I am alone, truly alone and can never go back to who I was. He was my only child, Lord, I gave birth to him and he was part of me, the only part of Allen and I together, which made us a family. Now I have nothing!* The more I thought about it, the harder I cried. It was one thing to lose a husband, it is quite another to lose a child. But to lose both is more than anyone can bear.

In spite of these thoughts, I cried out between sobs,

"Lord, I need You now. I am afraid of the days to come and of the loneliness and devastation in my life. I am broken beyond repair and without hope. All I know now is that I need You, Jesus, like I have never needed You before. I cannot do this without You, Lord. You are the Alpha and the Omega, the beginning and the end. I am broken to the point I want to die. Please, help me! I am not angry this time, Lord, just without strength to face the future and I will not survive if You do not help me." Saying it out loud into the stillness somehow comforted me.

In spite of my profound sorrow, I began to sense that God was listening and would be with me. While it did not stop my tears, I began to feel hope in the deepest recesses of my heart as I sensed a tiny bit of assurance that He would help me and somehow keep me from sinking into total despair in the days to come.

There is a despair so deep, only God can make sense of it. Where there was anger before, I was almost driven to trust God this time around. Where I had felt loneliness and devastation, there was a determination to let the Lord help me and comfort me. The reason was not that I had suddenly gotten so spiritual, but I knew without a doubt, that without trusting in Him, I would not survive. After Allen died, it was as if I had been thrown overboard into the waves of grief and tried to swim back to shore in my own strength. This time, I somehow had the feeling, if I laid on my back and looked up to the sky and let the waves carry me without struggle or effort, I would make it.

That first night, alone in my bed, amidst tears and pain, I knew I could not do it on my own. Like a little sheep, caught in a mighty storm in the middle of the ocean, I decided to let His love carry me to the shore and back to safety. It is not that I thought all this through, but when the storm takes on this magnitude, there is no purpose or sense fighting it, but just run for shelter in order to survive.

I truly believe the Lord had prepared me to trust Him while I was laid up in bed for all those months. I had developed a close relationship with Him and so was able to trust Him to help me. After all, He had brought me through the grieving process the first time, He would not leave me now. The words He spoke to me in the hospital this morning resounded in my mind over and over again, I WILL NEVER LEAVE YOU NOR FORSAKE YOU.

I did not understand why He took my boy, and I never will, but I knew He would be with me. It was as if this grief was so overwhelming, I had to give myself over to Him without hesitation, because to hold on to it would have been like committing suicide in my soul. I felt like that little lamb the Shepherd carried on His shoulders, because it was too weak, too broken and too devastated to take even one step on its own.

I cried most of the rest of the night as I gave my life over to the Lord. The enormity of my loss was too great to comprehend and so it was easier to cry and turn to Him for comfort. He had become a familiar friend to me over the last few months and it was this closeness I had developed with Him, that made it possible for me to turn to Him at this time. Looking back, I am touched that He so tenderly prepared me for this day when He made me to lie down in green pastures and experience His goodness and mercy all those weeks. It was not the 'normal' I had so desired that had brought me close to Him, but the quiet time spent with Him in His Word as my broken ankle healed.

And during this night of devastating grief, I reaped the harvest of my forced confinement, which brought this close relationship with Him and the certain knowledge, He would never leave me nor forsake me.

"Blessed are those who mourn, for they shall be comforted."
Matthew 5:4

Chapter 13

Too Soon

Time only goes one way – forward. Once it is gone, it is gone forever. Only the memories remain. But with God there is no time. That is why He told Moses, when asked His Name, I AM that I AM.

The next day, when the house was filled with people who came to help me mourn, all I could say to them over and over, "Too soon, too soon". Micah should have had many more years to live. Did God make a mistake?

But with the Lord there is only His perfect will at the perfect time. Since He does not divide time into hours, days and years in eternity, there it has no meaning. And for us, it does not start when we are born, but at the moment God created us, and neither does it stop when we die.

On that day, I measured my time with my precious son as way too short and could not fathom God's way was right or that He had planned it that way. Knowing this, He provided family, friends and neighbors for comfort and support who stood with me once again and allowed me to openly grieve.

Trying to understand God's ways is impossible for man, and any attempt to do so leads to nothing but frustration. Instead, He asks us to have faith and trust Him to know what He is doing. Because in time, more often than not, we will understand and are allowed to see even the 'why'. And when we do, this always leads to the realization of how much He loves us.

Corrie Ten Boom, a Holocaust survivor, author and evangelist in her eighties, shared how the Lord showed her how He looks at our lives. She held up a needlepoint from the backside. It was a mess of strings, lose threads and presented a picture of total confusion, chaos and made absolutely no sense. In her words, this is how we see our life when tragedy happens. Slowly, she turned the needlepoint until the front became visible and there, to our astonishment, was a perfectly beautiful, intricate picture of a peaceful landscape. And that is how the Lord sees our walk with Him. True faith is to be able to trust Him to make beauty out of our life, when all we can see is a mess of confusion and chaos. In other words, He knows the true picture of our time here on earth, since He is the One who wove the finished product.

Later in the morning, my boss, Dr. Weiss and his wife came. He was a dentist and she a psychiatrist. They offered to prescribe medication if I needed it and to stay until all my family arrived. I so appreciated their genuine concern and willingness to help, but told them my family was on the way from Alabama.

When they did come, I rushed into my mom's arms and once again, in her calm, reassuring way she found the right words to say,

"We're going to get through this, girl, so hang on and just trust God. Micah was my wonderful grandson and a good child. I loved him so much and remember the summers he spent with us on the farm during school break." Her voice was strong and filled with love as I hung on to every word. They made me feel better and we had a good cry together while holding on to each other. Her presence helped me sleep better that night.

One by one the family arrived and the house was filled to capacity with people who made me feel loved. The neighbors and church folks came through once again with food, cards and their genuine love during this time. My friends Keasley, Alice and Carol took care of organizing everything. The rest is a blur. All I remember, my unimaginable grief was lessened by the love and care of those around me during this time. I allowed myself to get lost in their compassion and so was able to function doing what had to be done.

I had to pick out the clothes Micah was going to wear. As I stood in front of his closet, I began to tremble. How many times had I picked out something for him since he was a child? And how often did he protest that he would rather wear something more 'cool'? That's when it came to me, why not let him wear one of Allen's jackets? It would make him proud to have on his father's best outfit for this special occasion. After all, he had tried so hard to fill his shoes during the last two years.

With sadness, I had agreed to plastic surgery for his face, since it was totally mangled on one side during the accident. Mercifully, they had turned his head in a way I could not see it when I stood with him in the hospital. I sent my brother John to check on the results. He came back telling me they did a good job, but he didn't look like Micah anymore. Kevin, Keasley's son went and sat with Micah at the undertaker until they closed and his devotion touched my heart.

I wanted to remember my boy the way he looked and did not go see him, but told everybody else they could view the body at the funeral home. I decided it would be a closed casket service.

The morning of the home going, I spent making a collage of Micah's pictures from the time he was six months till his college days. It would be placed at the front of the church for everyone to see. My heart was heavy, but at the same time I remembered this wonderful child the Lord had given Allen and I. He had been a joy and a good son in every way throughout his short nineteen years. How I would have loved to be at his college graduation and rejoiced with him over his first real job. How proud I would have been at his wedding and the birth of his first child. What comfort he would have been to me in my old age. And now I was alone! The tears began to flow as I arranged the pictures, dreaming of what could have been and never would be. An overpowering feeling of finality overwhelmed me with a force that was breathtaking. MICAH WAS REALLY DEAD! He would never come bouncing through the front door or grin at me as he kissed me on the cheek with his standard remark,

"Don't worry, I got this, Mom."

"Never" seemed an ugly word, one that I couldn't bring myself to say out loud. And so in silence, interrupted only by my crying, I finished the collage with tender care, carefully choosing which memory of my baby to share with others.

It was then I remembered the police telling me how the accident happened. Micah was driving. As he came to an intersection, another driver ran a stop sign. Micah swerved into the oncoming lane and right into the path of a big dump truck. His friend Danny next to him survived the crash and at that time was fighting for his life in the hospital.

At that moment the doorbell rang. A beautiful flower arrangement was delivered.

"Where do you want me to put it, Ethel?" Mom asked.

"Who is it from?"

"I don't know the name."

I got up and took the card attached to the arrangement and my heart froze when I realized it was from the young man who ran the stop sign.

"I don't want this!" I cried out and handed it back to Mom. "How dare he intrude into my day. He is the one who killed my boy, I don't want anything from him. I hate him for what he did!" I felt cold and bitter and empty when I looked at the beautiful flowers. *They can never bring him back, can they?* I asked with anger in my heart.

"Ethel, I know this is hard, but it is better to forgive this young man than hold a grudge. I am sure he is suffering terribly for what he has done. Let's let God judge him and then ask Him to have mercy. Remember, Jesus died on the cross for him and paid for his sin, just as He paid for yours. Un-forgiveness will harden your heart and bring turmoil into your life; forgiveness will bring healing. You may not be able to do this right now, but at least turn the young man over to the Lord with your willingness to forgive. Can you do that?"

I rushed to her and flung my arms around her neck.

"This is so hard, Mom, I don't think I can do it on my own."

"I will help you, child, we'll do it together." She took my hands and led me in a simple prayer for the Lord to bless the man who killed my son. I tried very hard to agree with her and obey her wise advice, but it would take many months until I was finally able to do it on my own with a willing heart.

When a tragedy like this has been caused by someone's actions, it takes a supreme effort to forgive. Yet it is this act of forgiveness that will lead to healing. And while it does not necessarily involve the right feelings, it is an act of obedience and a clear choice to follow God's commands. This has nothing to do with letting the guilty person get off free, but of releasing them to the Lord. By doing this, we are set free to overcome the tragedy in a way thatwill allow us to go on with our lives. Un-forgiveness may make us feel better in the short term, but it will eventually put us in a prison of hatred and bitterness from which we cannot escape unless we forgive.

It seems a harsh commandment Jesus spoke when he said,

"For if you forgive men their sins when they sin against you, your heavenly Father will also forgive you. But if you do not

forgive men their sins, your Father will not forgive your sins."
Matthew 6:14

Jesus in no way tried to say that I did not have reason for my un-forgiveness. What He is saying is, it is a sin if I am not willing to stop sinning. He cannot forgive me, since His forgiveness follows my repentance and repentance means to turn around and go in the other direction. In other words, if I want to be in right standing with God, I have to start with forgiving those who have hurt me.

Forgiveness is the only ointment that heals the terrible wounds of hurt when someone has wronged us. Un-forgiveness causes the hurt to fester inside and keeps us from healing. We can bury it deep down, we can try to forget it or ignore it, but it will still be there, surfacing at unexpected times and in surprising ways. Many lives have been spent in despair, pain and agony because people could not forgive.

God gives us a grace period and will always love us even if we cannot forgive, but the consequences He will not remove. While He will not withhold His blessings, the enemy will make sure we are not able to receive them since our communication with the Lord is clogged with feelings of bitterness and anger. It is not God who turns away, but it is our heart that turns away from Him.

This is why He tells us to forgive, so we can stay connected to Him unhindered and so overcome, heal and start a new life. In the end, we choose our future path, God will not force us. His Word gives us the guidelines for daily victorious living, yet He does insist we do it His way, because no other way works.

In the midst of my terrible grief I was guided by my wonderful, wise mother to do the one thing that would open the way to my full recovery. I had no idea then that is what I did, but in time I understood and it helped me tremendously to overcome and have the victory. The Lord was with me in His loving, wonderful ways even during this time and never left me even for a moment. It is only then I was able to look back and see His love and tender care He had for me in these most difficult circumstances. He did carry me, His little sheep, on His shoulders and I was safe.

The most memorable thing of the home going service was the response of the many young people who answered Bishop Morris' call to salvation. Micah was home and he would see them again in eternity because of his death.

"Why are you downcast, O my soul? Why so disturbed within me? Put your hope in God, for I will yet praise him, my Savior and my God." Psalm 42:5

Chapter 14

Irreplaceable Loss

We were never designed to grieve, that is why it is so hard. Think about it, when the Lord created Adam and Eve, they were supposed to live forever. Paradise was a place created for them for eternity without death, decay or loss of any kind – until sin entered. It changed everything so that since then, everything dies. EVERYTHING.

Well, not quite…

When the Lord created man in His own imagine, man's spirit will either enter the place called heaven or a place called hell. Another word for this death was eternal separation from God and it is irrevocable.

Well, not quite…

God made a way. The moment we accept the sacrifice Christ paid on the cross for us, His Spirit and ours are sealed together for eternity. And since God's Spirit cannot die or go to hell, neither can ours. We belong to Him forever, just like Adam and Eve once did - until they decided to go a different route - sin. This is the Good News Jesus came to earth to die for when He paid the price for our sin. The moment He said on the cross 'It is finished', He meant it. Unlike those who reject Him, we have been released from paying the debt we owe and are free to join Him in His Kingdom and live in fellowship with Him for all eternity. Just like Adam and Eve were supposed to do before they messed things up.

The bad thing is, after we accept the Lord we still mess up. Does that mean we are heading for hell – again?

Well, not quite…

Jesus paid our debt in full – past, present and future. Can we now sin to our heart's content? Of course not, but when we do wrong in spite of how hard we try, our ledger in the Book of Life will always show we are in the black. There is no red, because it was cleansed by His blood and our balance will only show zero – nothing is owed. NOTHING.

This is the essence of Christianity, called the Good News. It was first preached by Christ Himself in the first recorded words of His ministry,

"Repent, for the Kingdom of Heaven is at hand." Matthew 3:2

Contrary to popular belief, God is a logical Being. Since He did not design me for grieving, by accepting Christ, Allen and Micah are not really lost to me. I will see them again and spend eternity with them. Therefore, I do not have to spend the rest of my life grieving. This logical reasoning of faith is the ultimate antidote to grief and if applied, makes the difference between the world and a believer, between a future of hope or a life of hopelessness.

How I wish I could have been at that place of logical, godly reasoning on that day. When I stood in the cemetery, among the many people who had showed up on that early morning, I felt that the loss of my wonderful boy was irreplaceable. I am sure if I had stayed to watch the casket go into the ground, I would have collapsed or screamed or done something horrible. There was something so hopeless, so terribly final to think he was gone forever and buried beneath that dirt, my mind simply could not accept it at that moment. That is when I turned to those who stood there with me, my family and friends, neighbors and church family. It was as if they held me up with their love and comforting words. Just knowing my Mom was there, gave me strength as I drew on her faith and reassurance as she took my hand in hers during the beautiful service.

The repast was served by the Helping Hand Ministry of our church and for some reason, I still remember the delicious southern country breakfast they served. I was surprised how many had come and it comforted me.

The following week I was surrounded by my family. What a comfort, love and support I received and I wished they could have stayed forever. Yet all too soon, everyone had to return to their own lives. I remember the day when I waved goodbye and walked into my empty house. For the first time in my life I experienced that silence can be louder than noise. I would have given anything to hear

Micah call my name or ask what we are having for lunch or dinner. The house suddenly seemed so big and I felt so small as I walked into the kitchen to clean the dishes left over from breakfast. The stillness was deafening. I turned on the radio to my favorite Christian station and allowed the words of the songs fill my heart as I prayed,

"Lord, it's me again. What am I going to do now, please help me to know where to go from here. I am broken and lost and I am afraid." I started to cry and let the tears drip into the dishwater. What did it matter. I was alone now, nobody cared if they did. The loneliness was crushing and I was glad I had the dishes to wash, anything but sit down and think right now.

It seemed almost cruel that I was expected to go on with my life. How could I possibly do that? I was given four weeks off from work to get my bearings, but at that moment, I was sure I would never be able to return to a normal life. Nothing was normal anymore nor would it ever be. I WAS ALONE and would always be! "Lord, please help me face the future. I will not make it without You. You promised me You would never leave me nor forsake me. I have no choice but to believe Your Word. Help me to not just know it and believe it, but I also want to feel it in my heart. Please, let me feel it so I can go on."

I stood at the kitchen sink, waiting for Him to answer as the tears kept coming. Suddenly, I could understand when the Lord cried out on the cross, "Father, why have You forsaken me?" Jesus knew the Father had not left Him, but He just couldn't feel it. That's how I felt. *Lord, I know You love me, because of the way my family and friends have shown their love through all of this. I felt their love, I want to feel it in the same way from You.*

In the days following, the silence in the house was the worst, with no noise unless I made it. Instead of Micah's laughter, there was only my crying and sadness and it felt eerie. I knew I had to do something or I was not going to make it. It was getting harder each day to get out of bed. All I wanted to do was crawl back under the covers and pretend everything was as it had been before Allen and Micah had died. I was a wreck of self-pity and felt my soul had died.

As I stood one day and looked out of the window, filled with feelings of loneliness and grief, I watched the neighborhood kids playing hoop at the end of the block. A sudden, fierce anger at God washed over me as I looked on.

You have been to my house before, Lord and took my husband and now You have taken my son. Look at those kids. Some of them are not near as good as my Micah was and some are even bad. And yet You took him. Why not one of them?

My fierce anger at the Lord and the kids made me feel ashamed and I cried in part because I was sorry and in part because Micah wasn't there with them and never would be again. I knew it was wrong and at the same time I wished they would not be there for me to see.

I loved those kids. *Please, Lord, forgive my anger at them and at You. I am wrong, but this is so hard. I would give anything just to have Micah back for a little while just for one more time. Will my heart ever mend?*

I found out just how wrong I was in the days to come when these same kids raked my leaves, mowed my lawn and helped me in every way they could to show me how much they understood and cared.

There were two other people who showed me how much they cared by sending me cards and notes of comfort each week. Sallie and Juanita had no idea what their loving, kind words meant to me during this time. The Lord was truly using them to show me He cared and so did they. I eagerly waited for them each week. It is those little things that mean so much and can make the difference between hope and despair.

Finally, one morning, I made the hard decision to sort out Micah's clothes. With a heavy heart I entered his room and was almost afraid to touch his things. As I started, a thought came to my mind. Why don't I put his many baseball hats on display and let his friends come by and pick the one they would like to take for a keepsake to remember him by. The first friend I called was Frankie. He came and took one. Later, several others of his buddies from school and the neighborhood each picked a hat and promised they would wear it when they played and would remember him.

Amazingly, this made me feel good, knowing they wanted something of his to keep him alive in their hearts. This experience showed me I should give the rest of his clothes to the men's shelter. It made me feel good when much later, I saw some in the church wearing them.

One of the best ways to overcome grief or any other problems is to give out of that need. It had always been strange to me why the Lord in His Word asks us to give first and then it will be given to us. Now I understand. Instead of turning inward in our trial, our heart heals much faster when we turn outward and share what little we have with others. The Lord seems to want us to be willing to give until we have nothing left. Only then can His love, provision and comfort completely fill our heart. Holding on to what we have, just means there is no room left in it for what He has for us, which is so much better.

"Give and it shall be given to you." Luke 6:36

It is hard to experience God's ways are not our ways, especially when we are in the midst of hard times. It makes no sense according to our natural senses to reach beyond ourselves to others, but it is the best remedy for overcoming and healing. This may sound illogical and almost cruel for God to ask us to do, but it works.

Grief concentrates on how we feel; giving of ourselves to others concentrates on how they feel. Turning inward, while necessary for the first stages of grief, turns into a festering wound if allowed to continue over an extended period of time. Anger and bitterness have a way of increasing the pain, while forgiveness and giving to those who are worse off than we are, assures healing and hope in the long run, even in the midst of our own suffering. If we allow ourselves to reach out with the understanding we gained from our own pain, we are so much more able to give the compassion, love and empathy they are so desperately looking for.

That is what the above scripture means by 'give and it shall be given to you'. It is one of God's amazing principles that makes no sense until we obey it and then watch the wonderful results it brings. Looking back, my desire to share with others and help them overcome, helped me to heal and find the purpose in my life and make sense out of all the tragedy I experienced.

"If anyone would come after me, he must deny himself and take up his cross and follow me. For whoever wants to save his life will lose it, but whoever loses his life for me will find it."
Matthew 16:24-25

Precious Memories

The Butterfly Memorial in my Backyard

Chapter 15

The Butterfly

T here are many different ways God shows His love when we are grieving. In spite of our anger, pain or even bitterness, He loves us anyway. One of the hardest things during the four weeks I stayed home from work was watching the kids playing on the street in my neighborhood. Seeing them sitting on the curb, running, shouting and laughing, caused anger and frustration to rise up in me each day. I was not angry with them anymore, but that they were there and Micah was not one of them.

One day, as I turned into my driveway, I blew my horn at them when I saw them playing basketball as if nothing had happened. How dare they ignore my pain and enjoy life right in front of my house! I opened the garage door and drove in, but not before I glared at them. Before I could close it, my neighbor, a minister, walked over and with a gentle voice said,

"You know, they loved Micah, too."

I felt terrible, but could not find anything to say in return and went inside, crying. I knew I was wrong feeling this way again, but I didn't know how not to. My guilt increased when two of those same young men took turns to cut my grass over the summer.

As fall approached and the leaves started falling, I walked out one morning and the same sudden anger came over me. This time not at the kids, but at Allen and Micah.

How could you guys leave me with this mess? How am I going to rake those leaves when that has always been your *job?* I kicked the leaves with my foot. *How can you expect me to handle everything by myself, when this is what you are supposed to do? Nothing is the same, everything is on me and I am tired of handling it all.* A picture of the two of them enjoying themselves up there with the Lord came into my mind. *Right, you guys are playing the harp with the angels and sitting on a cloud having a good time, while I am down here raking leaves. Can't you see there is something wrong with that picture?*

I never had to rake, because once again, Micah's friends came to the rescue. And once again, I had to ask the Lord to forgive my outbursts of anger and frustration. Yet in spite of it, He supplied all my needs and loved me right through it all.

One day, Frankie called.

"Mrs. Perkins, I had a birthday party yesterday. It was in the evening and my friends and I sat around outside when a butterfly came into the yard to where we were. It was unusual, because they don't come around in the evening. We tried to shoo it away, but it wouldn't leave. That's when I imagined this could be Micah trying to join us. I told the others and then said,

"Man, we see you, glad you could make it." We watched it for a while until it flew off. After that we spent the evening talking about Micah and how much we missed him." Frankie paused for a second and then added,

"I just thought you would like to know."

When I hung up the phone, I realized how the Lord had sent this little butterfly to remind all of us how wonderful Micah had been and how much he was still in our hearts.

"Forgive my anger and bitterness, Lord. Thank you for showing me I am not the only one grieving. Bless those young people and keep them safe."

Ever since then, I cherish the image of a butterfly. It helps me celebrate the memory of Micah every time I see it. It is such a little, insignificant thing, but God can show His love in the most unexpected ways.

Memories can help us overcome our grief or throw us into renewed despair. It is important to concentrate on the positive ones and remove, if possible, those places, objects or situation that throw us into despair. While the butterfly gives me joy and good thoughts to this day, the pictures on the wall of Micah going up the stairs in my house, brought nothing but tears each time I looked at them. At first, I felt guilty wanting to remove them, but after a while I decided to take them down. I simply could not deal with looking at my boy from the time he was six months old till his graduation every time I walked those steps up or down. It was a step in the right direction to live in the present and not the past.

A feeling of dread swept over me the morning I decided to clean Micah's room. It was another way to eliminate memories that were too painful to face every day. When I entered his room, I realized for the first time that I could not ever start a new life if I stayed in this house. The memories of Allen and Micah permeated everything and would never allow me to make a new life. It was just a fleeting thought that day, but one that I knew would not go away.

Once again, I wondered why God chose to take Micah instead of the young man who ran the stop sign. How does He choose those He takes home and those who He leaves behind?

Since then I heard a story based on true events that helped me greatly with this question. There was a man who was asked to choose between his own son and his friend. Both were in a situation where the authorities could save only one of them and so asked the man to make the decision. He thought for a while and then chose the friend. When asked why, he replied,

"My son knows the Lord, his friend does not. I would like to give him some more time to make the decision to accept Jesus before he dies so they can be together again in eternity."

After I heard the story, I was able to ask the Lord to reach out to the young man and save him. This prayer set me free from any unforgiveness I might have still had. I do not know anything about him, but I pray to this day that he might have found peace and forgiveness from the Lord by giving his life over to Him. This was another one of those small incidents the Lord sent so I might be able to go on with my life.

Soon it was time for me to go back to work and I had no idea how I was going to manage. It was one thing to be at home and be able to cry, pray or just sit in silence whenever I wanted to. It would be quite another to work eight hours a day and concentrate on what I was doing.

The first week was terrible. Everyone was very careful around me and gave me all the space they thought I needed. I saw the pity in their eyes and their effort to avoid talking to me, because they had no idea what to say. There were several times where I had to leave the room and run to the bathroom, turn on the water and flush the toilet, so they could not hear me cry.

In spite of the kindness and love they tried to show me, I felt alone as if in a cocoon, with me on the inside. This taught me a great lesson as I minister to people who have lost a loved one. There are some people who never wish to talk about their loss. Then there are others who are helped greatly if they do. One of the ways to find out which way to help a person who is grieving is to ask them the simple question,

"Would you like to talk about Micah?" or another, "How did the accident happen?" This leaves the choice up to the grieving person and lets those around them know what to do without saying the wrong thing. Everyone grieves differently, but it is up to others to find out how they wish to be approached.

After a day or two, I finally shared with some and let them know it was alright to talk to me about Micah and it would actually help me with my grief. To this day, I am grateful for my work place and the people there who were so kind, understanding and helpful during this time. There were many days I couldn't function properly, forgot things or fell apart emotionally so they had to send me home. I never sensed any reproach from anyone and only felt love and understanding. For those occasions I carried a roll of toilet paper in my car. There were times, I had no idea how I got home. Once again, the Lord was with me, just as He said He would.

My neighbor Carol, a kind and wonderful woman, watched my struggle and one day asked me to go with her to a support group for parents who had lost their children. At first I did not want to go, but she convinced me. When I got there, I was sure no one could possibly be hurting as much as I was and didn't bother to listen. Until a woman started sharing about the loss of her three small children. She was a physician and was unable to practice medicine anymore, because she was so filled with sorrow and grief. It shook me to the core as she began to share.

"My husband and I had made plans to go to dinner and had asked a family friend to stay with the children. Because of our jobs, we did not get the chance to do this often, but enjoyed this special occasion. When we returned, our house was in flames and our children were dead. We found out, our friend had put a scarf over one of the lamps in the kid's room and it caught on fire. By the time the fire trucks came, it was too late. Our children died from smoke inhalation." She looked at us in the room with a look of such sadness, it took my breath away. "If we had not gone out to dinner, my children would be alive today," she said in a voice without emotion. "Just one dinner," she added in a whisper and buried her head in her hands.

In that instant, my outlook of what happened to me changed. Who was I to think I was the only one who lost a loved one? I couldn't even imagine her grief and sorrow as I sat there in silence together with the rest of the group. I looked around the room and realized that each person there had a story, a tragedy and pain to share. We were not there to feel sorry for ourselves, but to help each other. It was the first time I shared my story with a group and in doing so, it helped me on the road to recovery. There is no way to lessen the grief, but it is easier to deal with if we share it with others, especially with those who have been where we are. This is where we find out that God is not the only one who truly understands, but sends us others who do as well. And it is this feeling of belonging to a group of likeminded people that helps to lesson our own sorrow, because there is always someone there who is worse off than we are. Somehow, this makes us feel grateful for our own circumstances and gives us hope and encouragement that we will make it and overcome.

Grief groups, as well as other support groups, are a powerful tool for anyone who has a problem they cannot handle by themselves. Not only are they not as expensive as a psychiatrist, they help us see the need in others that is even greater than our own. To be among those who suffer from the same trauma as we do, is something a doctor or counselor cannot always understand. Neither is medicine the answer, since many times it only covers up the real feelings we need to be able to express or hear from others. This doesn't mean medicine is wrong, but it would be better to try to reach out to others and learn how to deal with grief before we resort to it.

In these groups, the faith and perseverance of those we hear share their stories serves as a great encouragement and hope that we also can overcome and find a way to a new beginning. In time we may even be able to help others overcome their grief by sharing how the Lord has helped us.

During this first meeting, the seed was sown in my heart not to just concentrate on my own recovery, but use my experience to help others. While it would be quite a while before I could even think about becoming a grief counselor, this was the day I somehow knew, it was the purpose the Lord had for me in the days to come.

"And do not forget to do good and to share with others, for with such sacrifices God is pleased." Hebrews 13:16

...TO GLORY

Part Two

Chapter 16

A New Beginning

L asting change is barely noticeable at first. Subtle and gentle, it comes without fanfare or drama, until one day we realize it is there. The peace in our loss we so desperately longed for, strived for and dreamed about, has taken hold in our spirit. We don't know how or when, but looking back, we understand it happened when we stopped striving and learned to live with what is, and not what was lost.

This state of mind does not mean the absence of grief, but our sorrow is controlled by hope, acceptance and peace and the comforting realization that life goes on and we will be alright. We are no longer driven to overcome the loss, but are in control of it. In other words, the loss of our loved one no longer dominates our daily life, but we are now able to manage our feelings and actions in a way that makes the difference between existing and living.

One of the biggest differences is now we can see what is going on around us instead of allowing our own feelings to be dominated and controlled by our internal grief. It does not mean we were selfish during our time of mourning. This time is necessary to recover and heal and should not be shortened. The length of time we spend in this phase of grieving is different for everyone and does not have anything to do with how strong or weak we are. It is not measured by how soon we recover, but that we do it in a way that is lasting and healthy.

God is not in a hurry. He will wait for us with love and patience until we have arrived at this stage at our own pace. We ourselves are usually the ones who judge harshly when our recovery takes longer than we think it should, because we thought we were more 'spiritual'. To be spiritual in grief is to let the Lord heal us, to be immature is trying to do it ourselves. The more mature we think we are, the more difficult this is, since we try to live up to an image we like to portray to ourselves and to others. It is disappointing when we find out we are unable to trust the Lord and overcome in record time for all to see. It is this 'showing off' that hinders many seasoned Christians from allowing the Lord to bring them to the point of full recovery and healing. A better word for it is pride.

The day I heard the story about the woman who lost her three children in the fire, was the moment I realized I will make it. Listening to her and the others who were dealing with their grief in the same way I was, helped me put my own sorrow into perspective. This is when I knew I had to help others and share with them that God is able to bring them through this terrible time. It was the moment I opened my eyes and for the first time noticed other people needed me. Suddenly, I knew the Lord had given me a purpose for my life, a specific area He had for me. He wanted me to use my experience of losing the two most precious men in my life and be a channel of His love and compassion for those who need me.

This is what is called, "making lemonade when life seems to hand you a lemon". I did not just talk about it, but put this revelation into practice by continuing to attend the grief group. It strengthened my desire to become a grief counselor. After a while I chose a group closer to where I lived. Strangely, it met in the same hospital Allen died. At first, I was reluctant to go there, but then decided it was not the place that mattered, but the purpose. The group was facilitated by one of the medical doctors and Rev. Jenkins. After a while, we moved to the Medical Examiner's office, which was even stranger. But I was undeterred, because these meetings helped me so much, I knew I had to stay.

The longer I attended, the more I knew I wanted to start a grief group in my church. Rev. Wanda Jenkins took me under her wings and I started training under her capable hands. After a while, I attended courses at Temple University to get a solid foundation in the different stages of grief. In time, I was able to pursue and complete the course work in Grief Recovery and earn my certificate.

In October of 1991, four years after Allen's death and almost two years after Micah's, I was a part of starting a new grief ministry in our church with the blessing of Pastor Morris. The meeting was called 'Surviving the Holidays'. It was led by Rev. Jenkins. The turn-out was good and we felt that was a sign to continue. By January 1992 we started meeting on a regular basis. I served as an intern first and after that, became a facilitator, together with my good friend Joyce, whose son had been murdered and left to die in the streets of Philadelphia. The official name of the group was "Comforting Friends, A Ministry to the Bereaved". It was the first of its kind in the inner city of Philadelphia.

As time went on, we were able to help other churches by training people to establish their own grief ministries. This proved a great outreach to the entire inner city community. It was rewarding to help so many people as men, women and even children came to us, seeking to overcome their loss. The grief ministry at Mount Airy Church is still thriving.

I see now what God had in mind when He allowed my losses. It was His way of training me for the purpose He had chosen for me. Without it, I would have never wanted to or could have done what I am doing now. To see how He weaves my life, it brings comfort and security, because it makes me realize, nothing is by chance in His Kingdom. It helps me to see each problem in life not as a problem, but a challenge to find out what He wants me to learn from it. Life is a giant classroom and we are the students. We learn in two ways, one is from His Book and the other from life. If we know what the Lord says in His Word, we are prepared to put it into practice in daily living and be victorious in spite of the trials that are sure to come.

The more we overcome our grief, the larger the scope of our understanding of this principle becomes. At the beginning, we can only see our own sorrow, then progress to becoming aware of other people's pain. From there, we are asked to advance by reaching out and giving of ourselves and minister to those who are where we once were. This stage is the end of true grief and the beginning of a new life.

Not everyone has to start a grief ministry to reach this point, but you can be there for your neighbor, your friend or the people in your church and workplace when there is a loss. Whether large or small, the impact you can have on even one person in need, may make a huge difference in their life. With your help they will be able to overcome and go on with hope instead of living with pain, fear and sorrow. God did not allow your experience for you to keep your knowledge to yourself. He wants you to use it and so be an extension of His love, compassion and mercy in other's lives.

One of the most amazing principle in God's Kingdom is this: The only way you can increase, is by giving away what you have.

"For whoever wants to save his life will lose it, but whoever loses his life for me will find it." Matthew 16:25

Chapter 17

A House is just a House – or is it?

J had a choice to make. You cannot start something new unless you leave behind the old. Trying to keep both will never work, because the old has a greater hold on us.

I had felt it coming on for quite a while, until one day I decided to sell my house. It simply held too many memories. Allen and I had bought it together in 1971 and it had been Micah's home from birth. Surprisingly though, it was not a hard decision to call Larry, a realtor, who also happened to be one of the ministers at my church. It seemed, after some prayer, what the Lord wanted me to do.

There are many stories of people who had lost someone and then kept their rooms, clothes and everything they ever owned untouched for years. To build a shrine or an altar to express our grief is not healthy, but keeps us bound to the loss with chains made up of their possessions. For true grieving and remembering is done in our heart.

The choice to go on with life means to leave behind certain memories and items belonging to the one we lost. By choosing to do away with these, does not mean we have to forget. We are not designed by the Lord to forget those things we want to remember, because our brain won't let us, unless sickness takes over. To keep memories intact, does not require us to keep outward surroundings or possessions, because they are only things. Our mind and heart is perfectly capable to remember our loved ones without outward trappings. If we hold on to these, however, they can hinder us from starting a new life and going on to new beginnings by enslaving us with never-ending grieving to worship at the altar of old memories, forced on us daily by looking at those items.

In my training as a grief counselor, I had learned these principles and put them into practice by putting the house on the market. Weeks went by and nothing happened. Not one soul came by to even look at it and I began to doubt if this was God's will.

Please, give me a sign, Lord. I want to do the right thing.

A few weeks later, I attended a prayer breakfast. During ministry at the end of the meeting, the speaker looked over the crowd and said,

"There is someone here who is worried their property is not selling. Do not give up, the Lord says it is going to happen."

I took that word to be for me and started to praise God. Everyone there joined me and we had a good time giving Him the glory and thanks even before it happened. A week later, I had a buyer for the house. Everything was looking great until the day of the signing approached. I started crying uncontrollably. The enormity of what I was doing caved in on me and I realized my head was ready, but my heart was not.

Several days later, the deal fell apart and so did I. What I thought was so easy and necessary to do, I had tried to dismiss as a minor hurdle. I found out it wasn't. How gracious and kind the Lord was to give me a chance to say goodbye to my wonderful home in a way that would give me closure.

I put the house back on the market with a heavy heart. Somehow, I knew the Lord still wanted me to do it. The day the sign went back up in front of the house, I decided to walk from room to room and re-live the memories of the years of happiness with Allen and Micah. We had lived there for twenty years. I remember when Allen and I walked in and knew right away this was the one, a two-story house, sitting on a beautiful corner lot with trees and a nice yard. It seemed big, with three bedrooms upstairs and two baths. But it wasn't long after Micah was born, until it fit our little family perfectly.

I walked down the stairs in my memory walk, looking at where Micah's pictures had been. When I reached the living room, I remembered the many times we had the family or friends over. As I continued into the dining room, the memories of sitting at the big table and sharing a meal with them almost overwhelmed me. I could still hear Allen share his silly jokes and watch his bright smile when everybody laughed.

As I walked on into the kitchen, I imagined Micah sitting at the small eating area by the window, trying to finish his breakfast in a hurry before school in the morning. How many times I told him how important it was for him to have a good meal at the beginning of the day so he could learn better. I am sure it went in one ear and out the other. I even went down to the basement to the laundry area and from there stepped out through the door into the backyard. This was my house, my home and my memories. Could I really leave it all behind?

Would it help me with my grief or would it mean the end of my memories with Allen and Micah? I stood and cried, asking God to help me make the decision. Then I remembered the speaker at the prayer breakfast and the joy I had felt at her words returned.

Three weeks later, I found another buyer and this time I had no trouble signing the papers. I had gotten my asking price. Not only that, the new house I was buying, had dropped its price and I got a large check back at the closing. God's ways are always right!

My walk through memory lane had brought closure and it was well with my soul when I closed the door behind me on the day I moved out. Once again, I marveled at the way the Lord had given me a second chance to properly sever the ties to this house, which would forever remain a place of happy memories for me.

One chapter of my life was over and I was free to begin another.

The new house was located in Rydal, Pennsylvania. It was a ranch style with three bedrooms, a large picture window and a full wall fireplace in the family room. It even had a brick barbecue grill in the big back yard. It was a wonderful place to start over again.

The change was hard in spite of the nice place. I truly felt alone at times in the new surroundings and doubt and fear filled my heart. Change is always scary, because it is filled with the unknown. And it is the unknown that is hard to face head on, when our heart longs for security and safety in what once was. There were days I wondered if I had done the right thing moving away from my wonderful neighbors, who had been such a comfort and support over the last few years.

With a sense of apprehension, I found out that I was the only person of color in this new neighborhood. I had never thought about that when I bought the house. I wondered how or if I would ever fit in as I stood looking out the window onto the street. I suddenly felt very insignificant and small, being the new kid on the block. For many days I stood and watched from different windows, until one day, I saw a woman sitting by the pool in the backyard. I mustered all the courage I had, said a short prayer and walked over to her.

"Hi, I am Ethel Perkins, your new neighbor," I said with a smile. She was an elderly woman. I couldn't tell whether she was smiling or not, because she held a tissue in front of her mouth. Nervously, I chatted on until I noticed she did not answer in any way. "I work at Temple University dental clinic; do you have a problem with your teeth?" I felt ridiculous, but I figured, because she covered her mouth the whole time, she had been to the dentist. It was the only thing I could think of to say when she didn't answer me.

At that moment, her husband walked out. He shook my hand and introduced himself and his wife. He was a retired judge and told me his wife had had cancer of the mouth and lost most of her tongue. He explained to me she could not talk and only went out with a mask over her face.

I felt terrible and at a loss for words, until I saw her eyes looking at me in a pleading way to stay. Over the next few months, I learned to decipher her words when she tried to talk in a very slow, labored way. I found out, I was the only person, except her husband, who understood her when she spoke. In time, she confided in me and told me of her cancer and how she could only eat food from a blender. Because of the deformed features of her face from the surgery, she rarely went anywhere and was glad to have me for a friend.

My house bordered on a deer sanctuary. While this was wonderful for me, my old neighbor on the other side, an avid gardener, was frustrated to no end with the many deer using his crops as a welcomed snack. In spite of putting a fence around the vegetable beds, the nimble animals had no trouble jumping over it and helping themselves during the night. I listened patiently to his complaints over most of the summer and fall. His wife apparently did not have near the understanding and relied on me to show enough compassion for two.

After a time, the old man died suddenly. It was then I was able to minister to his wife and share about my grief experience and how the Lord had dealt with me the whole time. Her husband's death brought back strong memories of Allen and Micah. Many times, while showing compassion, love and faith in ministering to her, I dissolved into tears the minute I returned to my house. I was stunned by the strength of my feelings of grief and sorrow, especially, since I had been sure I was past that stage.

I found out that grief has a way of surfacing when we least expect it. It seems it just gets covered up by a thin layer of skin, ready to emerge at any time. This is when I missed my old house and my old neighbors. I could have just called them and they would have showed up at my door with a pie or homemade cookies. But now, I was the strong one, the one who was expected to comfort and pray. It was a role reversal I hadn't realized I was supposed to be ready for, but the Lord was ready to use me!

The subject of race never came up in the new neighborhood until the lady from across the street asked me about it one day. We met every day while shoveling snow in our driveway and had become quite friendly. She was single, like me, and had a straight forward way about her when she asked me if I had ever encountered a backlash from the neighbors. I could not think of any and started to say no, when I thought about the incident with the police a few weeks after I moved into the neighborhood.

There was a big tree in my front yard, which leaned precariously toward the house. Since most of the homes sort of looked alike, with well-kept lawns and trimmed bushes, that tree was my landmark in the dark. The day after it was cut down, I was coming home quite late from a meeting. I somehow could not find my house and drove up and down the street several times in total confusion. That is when I saw the police car come up behind me and stop me. He asked for my driver license and registration.

"What are you doing in this neighborhood?"

When I told him I lived in the neighborhood and couldn't find my house, he looked at me with doubt until he checked my address on the license and then smiled.

"Mrs. Perkins, please follow me and I will take you home."

My first impulse was to think he stopped me because I was black. Later I realized, he could not have possibly seen what color I was through the windows at night. It made me feel better. After all, a car driving up and down our street late at night several times, looks suspicious and the policeman had just done his job.

I was beginning to settle into my new home and my new life and the Lord was with me.

"As for me and my house, we will serve the Lord."
Joshua 24:15

Chapter 18

Memories of Micah

Micah Allen Perkins
High School Graduation in 1989

hile some things, reminding me of the two people I loved the most, were necessary for me to get rid of, like my house, the memories of those who shared my love for Allen and Micah will never be forgotten.

In this chapter I would like to share how Micah's life impacted those who called him their friend. After all these years, their memories are vivid and real and a true testimony to the influence his short life had on others and I will treasure them forever. Would it be that all of us leave behind such a powerful testimony. Following are excerpt of what they answered when I asked them to write their thoughts down for this book.

Danny Curberson

I knew Micah since first grade at Cedar Grove Christian Academy. We were in the same class for pre-High School and High School. He was one of my closest friends. Our group of friends was unique. It is not many people who get to have a large group of close friends who have known each other almost their entire lives. (more than 20 friends).

Micah had a personality that everybody gravitated to and it transcended color, gender, religion etc. Our private high school was a potpourri of races. I didn't know anyone (teachers or students) who did not thoroughly enjoy Micah's presence. His infectious laugh and playful spirit kept us "in stitches".

His protective character always kept away those who didn't have our best interest at heart. I can't help but feel that trait had something to do with why I am still alive today. I was the one in the car with Micah when the accident occurred and I would like to share what happened on that fateful day.

After saving our money all summer, we decided to go to the mall since there was a big sale. On a slightly rainy day and after stopping at the bank, we set out with wads of money stuck in our pockets. (At least it looked like 'big money' to us). In Micah's slightly used black Mercury Cougar, we headed down Stenton Ave to the mall. The street has a steep incline with a hill on one side and houses on the other. There is a cross street at the bottom of the hill. As we approached the bottom, a Jeep Cherokee ran the STOP sign from the cross street, stopping at the double yellow line. Micah reacted quickly by swerving into the oncoming lane. As he turned to get back into our lane, he hit the brake. With the road still wet from the rain, the car fishtailed and we were hit by a 3-ton truck carrying 10 tons of gravel at full speed. Our car was knocked backwards, slamming into the Cherokee we had just avoided.

I firmly believe that Jesus first and then Micah's protective nature ensured that I am alive today by making sure that at least my side of the car didn't suffer the head-on impact. Because of my closeness to Micah, I refused to leave until the "jaw of life" had cut the car open and I saw them putting Micah into an ambulance. That's what brothers do for each other and I know Micah would have done the same. Sadly, he didn't survive the accident and was pronounced dead about an hour later in the hospital.

Micah was a brother and I miss him. I wish he was still here and I know our best friends feel the same as evidenced by the stories that still surface today, reminiscing about Micah and our adventures. He will never be replaced and will always be remembered. Can't wait to see him in heaven!

Danny graduated from Liberty University with a B.S. in Biology and Chemistry and is now a Director at a fortune 500 company and has the opportunity of playing an integral role in providing different vaccines that save so many lives globally.

Rita Milburn-Dobson

When I first met Micah, he was a cute boy with beautiful brown eyes. As I watched him grow up, he became a handsome young man; still with beautiful brown eyes. As his youth leader, I was devastated when I learned of his death.

I was a professional who dealt with life and death daily and yet this shocked me to my very core to the point that I felt helpless in helping the youth dealing with this tragedy. I was also unable to help Micah's mother who had lost her husband less than two years previously, and quite honestly, I felt helpless in dealing with my own grief as well.

However, Micah's death and how ill prepared I was in dealing with it helped me pursue additional information on the topic of death and dying. This eventually helped me to form a non-profit organization which assists children and teens in dealing with death and bereavement.

Rita Milburn Dobson
Micah would often joke about how much trouble he was NOT able to get into, because he had a praying mother. He shared that sometimes he was about ready to get into some "trouble with his friends", but something stopped him. He told me he would get mad when he couldn't do it, because "Every time I turn around she is praying for me."

His mother must have known through discernment that he needed ore prayer and we would laugh about it.

I thought of you, Ethel, when I wrote this today:
In our own grief we can become a source of life for others.

Frankie – now SSGT Frank Tucker III
My relationship with Micah will always have an indelible place in my heart. After our fathers passed away, we began to spend a lot more time together. Neither of us complained, but we knew that our lives had changed completely. We never spent a lot of time on dwelling on their passing, but more so on what we needed to do to become successful in our lives. Micah was the one who kept me grounded and focused on doing that by talking about our future plans and how we could plan on achieving them. We both decided not to give our mothers any problems and help out with finances and things around the house and fill the shoes our fathers left behind. Doing it together made it a lot easier. There is a comfort when you know that you have someone feeling the same things you are, but even more so when it is a lifelong friend.

I never heard Micah ask why his father was taken away or why God chose to do this to him. His faith was steadfast in Christ and he never wavered from that. We did stumble and found ourselves in trouble sometimes, but we bounced back on the right path with the guidance of our mothers.

The day I found out he passed was rough. I found comfort in knowing that we had had something special and there was no question that we loved one another as brothers in Christ should.

It is not just Micah who has touched my heart, but you, Mrs. Ethel Steedley. The average person would have fallen apart, losing their spouse and only child, but you got stronger. Having you and Micah in my life has truly been a blessing for me. You have shown me that when God has a plan for you, He has a plan for you. Run the race and He will let you know when it is finished.

Greer Thomas

There are so many memories I have of my dear bud, Micah. We were truly great friends, even though many thought we were dating. Micah was a cool, calm, relaxed, playful, adventurous, daring, and yet shy guy. At the same time, he was nice, caring and easy going. He always tried to have this serious face, but impossible, because you could see that little smirk on his face, which really was his smile.

We spent many hours talking on the phone about general things as well as deep, inner concerns or issues. Micah always confided in me.

I remember, it was a week before he died. I stood at the corner of Upsal and Stenton Avenue waiting for a bus, when he swung around the corner, rolled down the window and said, "You want a ride?" And then just starts laughing as he normally does and I hopped in. My last words to Micah was to slow down and do the right thing, not knowing, it would be the last time I would ever see him. It was the first time loosing such a dear and close friend at such a young age.

He will always and forever be a part of my memories. To this day, I still miss my best bud, Micah!

Juanita J. Byrd

Micah had a tremendous impact on my life by his godly character. He was very intelligent and kind in every situation or task given to him. Micah's social skills always impressed me; his smile was contagious, filled with much love and humility. I will always keep a special place in my heart for him. This helps me to remain at peace, knowing that he is with the Lord. I will never forget Micah, though he was only with us for a short time. He left an imprint on my life and on each member of my family.

Lu Chambers

I don't remember ever meeting my best friend Micah. That's because we grew up together in the same church. Micah was more than a friend to me, he was a brother. A year younger than me, he was the coolest guy I knew. He could make you laugh and could tell the most elaborate stories and make you believe it was true. I can't even recall how many times I spent the night or hung out for hours with my best friend. He had a great spirit and it was a joy to be around him.

I believe Micah could have been famous. He was so charismatic and talented in basketball and soccer. He also had an excellent hand when it came to art and sketching. But he wasn't cut out to be a barber, that's for sure. I know, because he gave me a haircut that made my mother look at me in horror and had me wearing a hat for weeks. Micah just laughed which made me laugh. Those were great times!

I vividly remember the day he died. It was a Friday and I was supposed to hang out with him. When he didn't show up, I walked up and down the block near my house, trying not to worry. After a while, I went back to my house. When I got the phone call that he had died in a car accident, my world caved in. I questioned God over and over again, why did He take my best friend and brother? It took many years for me to get over his death, because I wanted him to be alive!

In 1999, when my wife Deedra became pregnant with our first child, I asked her if we could name our son Micah. She knew how I felt about my childhood friend and agreed. When *our* Micah was born, I prayed and gave God thanks for helping me heal.

I dreamed about Micah many times and his legacy and the impact he had on my life will be forever in my heart. I look forward to the day we will reunite in God's presence.

Kelly Harris, Professor of African American Studies.
I have many fond memories of Micah. Most of them are sports related. Although all of the Rodney street children recall Micah's famous 'whupping'. It was a favorite thing for us kids to listen when someone was getting disciplined. In the end, we all caught our fair share.

Micah had a way of bringing his good nature to everything he did. I honestly don't remember him ever being upset or yelling to the point of anger. He loved to play basketball. There is one moment that stands out more than any other and is an example of his wonderful personality. I had polished my sneakers with bright white shoe polish before we went to play. My sneakers were old and beat up and I wanted them to look new. As we were playing, Micah was laughing his classic laugh when he saw the white streaks on my legs and shorts.

During the next break, when the guys asked about them, he told them they must have come from the chalk on the asphalt. He never gave me away and his imaginative explanation kept me from getting laughed off the court. He was a good-natured, decent loyal friend to the end.

It was due to Micah's suggestion I checked out the department of African American Studies at Temple University and got a greater sense of urgency about school and the program. Today I am a professor of African American Studies and I have my good friend Micah to thank for leading me there.

I must say, I miss Micah dearly. I spoke to him on the day of the accident. He told me he and Danny were on their way to Plymouth Meeting and I asked them not to play basketball without me. Micah, laughing, told me not to worry and they would pick me up to shoot some hoop. That was the last time I spoke with him.

Even though I was older than Micah and Danny, they were both outgoing and gregarious and that made it easier for me to socialize if they were in the room. I often think about Micah and wonder what he would be doing now. But I am never sad when I reminisce about him, because I know I am a better person for having had him as a friend.

Vanessa Chambers

How do you define a 'brother'? Micah and I may not have been connected by bloodline, but by heartstrings, nearly tied around common experiences and fierce loyalty. Born only four weeks apart, in the same church, and blessed with the same godmother, it was inevitable that our paths would not only cross, but also connect, intertwine and meld together.

What I remember most about Micah was his humor. He found the lighter side in every situation. Where there was none, he created it, often playing pranks, laughing at himself or causing others to laugh at his numerous antics. I still chuckle today when Micah gave my older brother a bowl haircut and was gone in time so he did not have to witness the fire in my mother's eyes.

I will never forget when my family visited the home when Micah's father died. Despite his own personal grief, he smiled and eased the tension and managed to be the encourager while the rest of us were the recipients. That was Micah's gift.

The day Micah died is clearly etched into my mind. It was the most devastating news to ever rock my world. At 19, I felt disbelief, shock and praying that this was only a dream. Sometime after Micah was laid to rest, his mother found a letter addressed to me among his things. It was a brief note, decorated with a colorful, original sketch, saying he would miss me when I was gone. How ironic. I was the one missing him terribly. I have treasured the note ever since.

Today, I am an educator and have taught several Micah's over the past 23 years. Whether they have his same jovial spirit or even carry his name, they continue to teach me the lesson I've learned from Micah: life is short, unpredictable, and should be celebrated with laughter daily. Most importantly, behind the laughter there is a heart of gold. Although his time with us was short, he has never been forgotten. My children, nieces and nephews have all heard the stories, seen the pictures, and know the 'uncle' they never had the chance to meet.

Dejay (Byrd) Ducket

We were just arriving home from a family vacation, when the phone rang. I answered it,

"Dejay, it's Greer's mom," the voice said quietly on the other end. "There's been a terrible accident and Micah passed."

My mind went into full denial for a second. Maybe it was another Micah and this was some kind of terrible mistake. OUR Micah, who had soft, smiling brown eyes and a hearty laugh that was infectious, was the one I had grown up with and who had played at my house. He couldn't be gone! I remember the time, not too long ago, when I had been in the choir loft watching him and his mother say their final good-byes to his dad. It was the first time I experienced the death of someone close to me who was my age; and it made me feel vulnerable. Many things changed for me that day, but I have never forgotten Micah, and I never will.

<u>Carolyn Crumbley</u>

I remember when Micah was learning the books of the Bible at school. I was and adult and had never memorized them. When I realized that little Micah knew them all it encouraged me to learn them from Genesis to Revelation. I thank God that young Micah to help me to do it. After all these years I still have to test myself to stay sharp. …And a child shall lead them.

It is good to listen to others reminisce about those we have lost. It solidifies our memories of them and brings with it a mixture of joy and sorrow at the same time. But it also brings healing to our soul to be able to share with those who knew them and the stories they have to tell. It brings comfort and joy to hear the love they have for those we love and spend time remembering together.

Memories, especially shared ones, have a way of helping us to overcome our loneliness, sorrow and grief. They bring our loved one back into our minds and hearts as we share their life, their laughter and special moments. That is why it is important to allow and even encourage others to share their memories with us. The joy this brings far outweighs the sorrow, because it creates a bond and a lifeline that helps us not to feel the loss alone.

Remembering Micah through the eyes of his friends has been a tremendous comfort and joy for me. It was good to find out they saw him the way I did, a wonderful young man, whose life mattered to others almost as much as it had to me. In reading these accounts, it amazed me what an impact Micah had on so many people and how much they loved him and still remember him. It brings a sense of closure and even joy to know, my son was a wonderful person, loved and appreciated by others.

At the same time, it makes me wonder what he would have been like as a grown man. I will never know, but then, the Lord knows and that is enough for me, because I will see him and Allen again in eternity.

"Death has been swallowed up in victory. Where O death, is your victory? Where O death, is your sting?" 1 Corinthians 15:54-55

Chapter 19

The Guilt of Recovery

rief is not supposed to last forever. When it has served its purpose of restoring us to a new normal, it should no longer dominate our thinking or actions.

After the many months of living with sorrow and emotional pain, it felt strange to experience an entire day without thinking about Allen or Micah. Was I starting to forget them? How could that possibly be?

Guilt washed over me as I lay in bed one evening. Did this mean I didn't love them anymore? These questions ran through my mind and I felt terrible. *Lord, is it wrong to have fun, wrong to stop thinking about them all the time? I have finally come to a point of enjoying life again. How can I possibly do that without them? What is wrong with me?* I knew I could not share those thoughts with anyone. What would they think of me? I felt confused. Was I disloyal or such a cold-hearted person to forget about my loved ones? Please Lord, help me sort this out.

Feeling this way is the result of successful grief, because to have reached this point is the beginning of the end of mourning. It felt strange, even uncomfortable and unsettling for me to realize, I could function without being influenced by grief. At first, guilt took the place of grief, replaced by a desire to stay in that familiar place of sorrow out of loyalty to Allen and Micah. I was sure I should not be this content with my new life as a widow and mother of a dead son and tried to force myself to think sad thoughts of loss and pain. I definitely would not want people to think I got over it and had stopped grieving. I did not even want to admit it to myself and tried very hard to squash those feelings of 'normal' in my heart.

This caused me to feel unsure of myself in my grief ministry. Maybe I wasn't qualified to teach others what I didn't have within myself. I didn't realize then, to teach others to overcome grief I had to overcome it in my own life first. We cannot give to others what we don't have. In other words, the only way I can pass on what it means to grieve, is to have overcome it and now live a normal life without it. A teacher has to have graduated from college before he can teach.

While still a student, he does not have the full range of knowledge to pass on to his students. That doesn't mean we don't know anything before, but it is not the same.

Most people seek out a grief counselor because they cannot handle their feelings during the initial shock of loss. Someone who is in the grieving stage themselves, cannot possibly help others in the same way as one who has come through it successfully, because they are not influenced any longer by their own strong feelings and emotions.

I was in that strange place of having graduated and then took my graduation as a failure. This guilt of having succeeded is another normal step in the journey of grief. What helped me overcome it was, I became active in the church in the missionary department, taught Sunday school and participated in the hospitality ministry as well took my place back as church announcer. I also kept up with the grief ministry. It was doing very well as it gave me a wonderful feeling of being able to help others overcome while helping me see it was alright for me to feel normal and enjoy life again. I began to travel with Rev. Jenkins across the city and other states and share my story.

As time went on, the feeling of guilt stopped and I was able to experience the joy of a new life without Allen and Micah. There was a freedom now to think about them without crying as positive memories replaced sorrow. I was able to smile when I thought about them and share about our life with others, feeling joy and gratitude to have had them in my life.

It does not mean that I don't have feelings of sorrow when special days and dates come each year. But I see my life now in a different way, filled with good memories and ready to face a new future without guilt. I started inviting friends over for dinner and fellowship. This is when I was glad to have a new dining room, because it would have still been a little hard to remember the days when Allen and Micah were still there.

The desire to change your surroundings is an important part of overcoming your loss. This does not mean you have to buy a new house like I did, but re-arranging your furniture, painting your rooms and hanging pictures in a different place, helps to start fresh. The place you shared with your loved one for so long is now your own; make it truly yours by redecorating. This is not to erase the memory of the one you lost, but to reaffirm your new life without them.

Another thing I did to celebrate my future was that I started to go to Broadway plays and even took a cruise with friends. While I no longer felt guilty, it was still a little hard when I remembered Allen was going to take me on one for our anniversary and never got the chance. At this point, the idea of getting married again never entered my mind. I was content with my single life and had a lot of friends who loved me and saw to it I was not alone.

When I decided I would not go to Alabama for the holidays, Denise, Keasley, Juanita and Winifred took turns inviting me to join their family for dinner during this time. I felt loved and thanked God for my wonderful friends.

Looking back, my outlook had changed. I felt like I was a new person, able to function on my own with God's help and the love of my friends. God had been there all the time, just like He promised. My walk through the valley of the shadow of death was over and I had come through it without the enemy destroying me. But it wasn't just my outlook that had changed, I had changed.

Going through something like this makes us either bitter or better, the choice is ours. To have experienced the range of strong, powerful emotions during this devastating time has made me a stronger person. Hopefully, it has also made me a better person, able to empathize and have compassion for those who are hurting. It brings to mind the scripture in Romans 5:3-5

"Not only so, but we also rejoice in our sufferings, because we know that suffering produces perseverance, perseverance, character; and character, hope. And hope does not disappoint us, because God has poured out his love into our hearts by the Holy Spirit, whom he has given us."

The guilt I had felt about my new life passed and I felt a wonderful freedom to live again. Unfortunately, there were still many days that brought the pain of loss. They came as sudden as a summer storm and were over just as sudden.

During this time, I had many dreams about Micah. In every one of them I was somehow trying to catch up with him, but never could. What was unusual about them, they were not sad, but happy. It was as if we were playing catch and he would laugh and run ahead of me. I thought many times what they might mean. Could it be that he was with the Lord, waiting for me to follow him, knowing it wasn't time yet? I would wake up with a pleasant feeling of having spent some time with him and it made me happy and help me get back on an even keel. It was the hope the above scripture is talking about, the hope to be with the Lord and my loved ones in heaven.

The Lord can speak in many ways and dreams are an important avenue of His communications with us. Of course, most dreams mean absolutely nothing, but when the same one occurs repeatedly or you wake up with it clearly in your mind, ask the Lord what it may mean. Just remember, any dream that is dark, gloomy and brings with it a feeling of doom and hopelessness, is never from the Lord. Also, if the dream goes against the principles of scripture, you may be sure it is not from God. The Lord will never go against His own Word. These dreams are nightmares and can be from the enemy to harass and torment you.

When we ask for a sign from the Lord, the one He gives us may not always be what we want to hear. But is essential that we hear His voice, especially during hard times. The best 'sign' is to read His Word. The Bible is not just any book, it is Holy Spirit inspired and therefore, His guide for daily living. To find out about God's character, the way He is, what He is and how He deals with us, is to read His instruction manual.

How can you possibly know God without knowing anything about Him? He is not shy about telling you and so wrote a very thick book called the Bible. If you find it hard to read, get one that is called The Living Bible or other modern translations. These are not meant for study, but for easy understanding and read like a story. To know all about Jesus, start out with the four Gospels called Matthew, Mark, Luke and John. All four tell of the life and ministry of Jesus from four different points of view, because they were written to different groups, such as Jews and Gentiles. While all were Christians and made up the early church, they had different backgrounds, customs and lived in different places of the world.

Another way to hear from God is through a sermon in church, TV or any other place. Many times, when I had a questions for the Lord, I heard the minister preach on the same subject the very next Sunday. How exited I get each time it happens, that this big, powerful and loving God would take the time to answer me in such a personal way. But the minister is not the only one God can use. Sometimes talking to your friends, neighbors or anyone else, they can say something that brings clarity to a question you have. God is very resourceful in His communication with us.

In the old testament there were many prophets who foretold the future, warned the Israelites and spoke to kings and normal people about God's will. Many will say, they don't exist anymore today. Why would God love us any less now? As a matter of fact, in 1 Corinthians 12:27-28 the Apostle Paul writes the following instructions to the early church,

"And in the church God has appointed first of all apostles (they establish new churches), second prophets (they speak for God), third teachers, then workers of miracles, also those having gifts of healing, those able to help others, those with gifts of administration, and those speaking in different kind of tongues."

It is exciting to hear from the Lord when you have asked Him a question. During times of grief, we are confused, scared and at a loss in every area of our life. That is when we need to hear from the One who has all the answers. Someone told me they asked the Lord, why He speaks in a small, still voice instead of a trumpet blast.

"So you REALLY have to listen when I speak to you."

So when I was uncertain whether to sell my house or not, He used the speaker at the breakfast meeting to prophesy that someone in the meeting was worried about selling their property. Not only was His word true, but He made it possible for me to have the time to do it in a way I had peace about it.

Two years after Micah's death, my church had a visiting evangelist. He asked me to come up front and prophesied,

"The Lord sees you and will restore what the canker worm has taken from your life. He will give you a new husband, one that is acquainted with death and sorrow and he will love you with all his heart."

At the time it seemed impossible and even ridiculous, because I had no intentions of ever getting married again. It would be fourteen years before the words of the prophet came to pass. God never lies and His Word can be trusted.

"But seek first his kingdom and his righteousness, and all these things will be given to you as well." Matthew 6:33

Chapter 20

Reaching Out

The final victory in overcoming grief is to reach out to those in need by sharing your own journey. No classroom or theoretical study on grief is as effective as what life has taught you. By having gone through the trials, pain and sorrow of losing someone, you have gained the personal experience necessary to truly share with sensitivity, compassion and understanding with those who are in the midst of it. Those caring feelings cannot be learned through books, but develop through having gone through the valley of grief and come out on the other side a stronger and more faith-filled survivor.

The turning point from grieving to sharing is the moment you have the desire to give of yourself by helping others instead of reaching out to receive. This point in your recovery cannot be rushed, but must develop gradually. It has nothing to do with being a good Christian, but rather having arrived at the point where the Lord is ready to use you. And only He knows when that time is. Everyone grieves differently and reaches this point at different times. But one thing is certain, no matter how long it takes, you should eventually get there.

This does not mean, you should not learn from those who are the "professionals", because they probably have been through it and then, through many years of experience, have learned the skill to council in a way that will bring the best results. After all, when I had reached this point, I realized I only knew how I grieved, but had no idea how others deal with loss.

This is when I decided I wanted to know more and learn from those who could teach me. In other words, I decided I wanted to become a grief counselor.

The first step in my desire was, I realized there was a need in my church for it. I had come to the point of looking past my own grief and on to others in my own sphere of life. I had reached the milestone of wanting to give instead of receive. This was not a certain moment, but it had started quite a while back, even after

Allen died, but got stronger when Micah passed. What made it certain was when I heard the woman in my first grief group that lost her three children in the fire and saw her overwhelming state of grief. I knew I couldn't help her at that time, but I was sure I wanted to help others like her.

This desire inspired me to talk to Pastor Morris about the need in our church and resulted in the birth of the 'Comforting Friends Bereavement Ministry'. But there was a lot to do before we could actually get started. We began by inquiring of Rev. Wanda Jenkins MHS, the director of the Grief assistant program with the medical examiner's office in Philadelphia. Together with several other church members, we started to attend her classes and workshops on subjects like Patterns of Grief, Different types of Grief, Social Factors affecting Grief, Do's and Don'ts for facilitating support groups, and workshops on Children's Perspective of Death.

It was a vigorous time of training at the Center of Urban Theological Studies, consisting of many workshops and classroom studies and were required for certification to complete our education.

This learning process taught me valuable lessons about the many forms of grief and how to cope. But more than anything else, it showed me that the Lord is the only One who can bring us through it successfully, no matter the human effort. All I can ever do is listen, share and be there for those who need me and then love them right where they are in their grief journey. God will do the rest.

We had our first special session in the church in November of 1991 with the subject of 'Getting through the Holidays'. Our first regular meeting took place in January of 1992. Our mission statement was: This is a ministry of giving comfort to the bereaved and to help them sustain themselves by giving them a helpful hand and letting them know they are not alone through practical and spiritual ways.

In time, we extended our program to include children in grief, facilitated by several degreed counselors. Additionally, the first year we were able to have many other professionals come and share their time with us, including the grief counselor for children with the Pennsylvania school system, a Family Therapist, a Pastor and the director of a Christian school. All these helped us to establish our ministry and put it on a solid footing in our community as it slowly became an anchor of comfort and help to the bereaved.

After a year, we received many wonderful, positive testimonies by those who had been helped through Comforting Friends Bereavement Ministry. What a joy and encouragement it was for all of us to know that we were truly making a difference in people's lives! I would like to share some of these and hope they will show how important it is to seek help when you feel alone and devastated in your grief.

Her name is <u>Vivian.</u>

She had lost her daughter Linda during childbirth. The doctors told her, since she had gone into seizures, that her child would be retarded. Since Vivian was an RN, she knew it didn't look good and the doctors were probably right.

"My daughter died the day after she delivered a little girl, but praise God, my little granddaughter was perfectly healthy and she is the joy of my life. Comforting Friends has been without a doubt a helping hand through this most traumatic and devastating time in my life as they wiped away my tears and helped me and loved me when I needed it the most. Anyone who has ever experienced the loss of someone so dear like my daughter was to me, can understand my anxiety, hurt and frustration during this time. Sister Perkins, along with others in the ministry, helped me to have the faith in God to guide me on the road to recovery. They all showed me love, tenderness and compassion during this heart-wrenching time by being there for me. I praise God for their ministry!

Her name was Iris Wiggins

Comforting Friends has truly been a blessing to my sister and myself. To us it is best described as a soothing balm for our wounded, grieving hearts after we experienced multiple losses in our family back to back within one year.

Comforting Friends is a place where we feel free to share with no judgment or pressure. Thank you for answering God's call to start this group that has helped many of us in so many ways. God bless you.

Her name is <u>Angela</u>.

She came to Comforting friends not because of the death of a blood relative, but because her best friend had died of a massive heart attack. She wanted to learn how to help her friend's six-year old son and his father, who were devastated by the loss.

"I knew I had to learn how to help this child deal with his mother's death and needed to find out how children grieve differently from adults by knowing about the grief cycles, their duration and that they get shorter as time goes on. I knew to let the child color and not be shocked by the dark pictures he drew at first, or allow him to act out through disruptive behavior without punishment at his mother's birthday or other memorable events. I also learned to nurture him and help him talk about his mother freely and just listen or ask gentle questions.

Since my initial focus was entirely on the child and his father, I never allowed myself to grieve during the next four months. It was when I had to go on a business trip and had to look for a babysitter for my daughter, I became real angry with my friend. She had always been there before and now she was dead. She had left me! I had always counted on her in times of need and was shocked at my strong reaction. It was when I shared with those at Comforting Friends, I realized, I was belatedly going through the first stage of grief I had talked about, but never allowed myself to experience. Because of talking to someone there, I did not get stuck in my anger stage, but overcame, praise God.

I also praise Him for leading me to Comforting Friends so I could find out how to care for others in many other circumstance other than just grief. Their comfort and advice have helped me to be uplifted and reach out to others during times of stress.

Her name is <u>Joyce</u>.

This ministry has been a blessing to me after the death of my mother and son in 1990. At the time I had no one to share my feelings with at my church until I talked to Sister Perkins. In spite of grieving over the death of her own husband and son, she reached out to me. We became friends and began sharing our desire to start a grief ministry together. Over the years we worked together until she moved on to Florida. Because of the training we took together, I became coordinator of Comforting Friends. After all these years, the ministry is still going strong, praise God!

Her name is <u>Barbara B. Burton</u>

Presently the Coordinator of Comforting Friends

When I joined Comforting friends 20 years ago after the death of my husband, to say I was lost would be an understatement. We had been married for 29 years. Despite what the doctors told me, I knew God would heal him. When he did not, I had no direction or desire for anything. Having been with him since the age of fourteen, I did not know how to be Barbara without my Burt.

Comforting Friends allowed me to cry when I wanted and to share when I needed to. I could talk, cry, yell or be quiet during the meetings and people understood. I could even say I saw or heard him last night and they could relate and empathize with me. I could tell them I still had all of his things in the exact same places and they knew why. I saw women of all ages who had been as lost as I was and who were trying to find their way out of grief by standing in faith; and I wanted to be able to do like they did.

Here I learned all about the different stages of grief, the tangled emotions, the effect grief had on me physically, mentally, emotionally and socially. I learned how many things I had done for my husband and my family to make them happy, things I really didn't like. I finally learned to pay attention to me and what I needed to be whole again.

I now coordinate the Comforting Friends ministry and am on the other side of the table, because I can put into practice those things that worked for me. The CF ministry is alive and well and still a much needed outreach for our community to this day.

One of the hardest interviews I ever had to do was with our youth pastor Walter Chavers. It was held during my training period and was part of my assignment before I was certified. Pastor Chavers was a young man and much loved by everyone in the church. The diagnosis of his terminal illness came suddenly and he had to make drastic changes in his lifestyle without much warning.

"I have made my peace with the Lord," he told me, "and know I am going to die soon. I cannot work any longer and have to stay home. I can still use the computer and so having time to help with the transfer to my successor. It is quite a new responsibility for me to turn over the running of this family solely to my wife Carla. That part has been hard, but we are managing. I know it is very hard for our two children to see me go from a healthy young man to this state. I hope I have been able to put their mind as ease when I told them I will be with the Lord soon and see them again in eternity. I have done all I know how to do to make it easier on Carla and the children. For the rest I put them into the Lord's hands."

This interview was very hard on me as I listened to this wonderful young man dealing with his own death. So I just sat there and mostly listened, asking only a few questions over the few days I spent with him. I had the feeling, being able to talk about it to someone other than his family, helped him somehow.

I was also able to share with his wife Carla and the children about what to expect after their husband and father was gone and it brought back many painful memories for me.

We had very few men come to our ministry. One stands out. He was a Bishop and had a mentally challenged daughter who lived much longer than expected. It was still heartbreaking when she finally died and he and his wife came to talk to us. It truly helped him, since men have a much harder time to share their grief. Instead, they usually hold it in and many times throw themselves into their work.

Most of the people we helped were Christians, who knew the Lord and were comforted by that fact alone. However, we had one young girl, twenty-one years old, who told us she was an atheist. Her name was Judy and she could not get over her anger for losing both of her parents at 18. It took us quite a while to help her get over her feelings of bitterness and rage at life, until, eventually, she improved enough that she decided to go back to school. To our delight, she earned a degree in grief counseling. But the day she finally accepted Jesus as her Savior was a day of rejoicing for all of us at the ministry.

There were many different ways we helped those who came to us. Some on a spiritual level, others in a more practical way. We had a mailbox at the church where people could leave us their name and number. We would then contact them by phone or visit their home, attend the home going or pray for them and share with them information about the ministry and the different ways we can guide them through this hard time. Those of us who attended our church, we sent cards or called if they did not show up for the service. Sometimes a visit to their home and find them depressed, lonely and overwhelmed. What a joy it was for them to know someone cared enough to reach out to them.

Rita, the facilitator for the children, made sure I received a card every anniversary of Micah's death for over five years. Usually all it would say, 'I remember Micah today'. It truly ministered to me that someone cared.

During this time, I had other major losses in my family. My father-in-law died two days after my fiftieth birthday. He had been in the hospital for several months, but one is never really prepared for the shock when it happens. I was able to help my mother-in-law in her grief and thank God I knew what to do to stand with her during this time.

A year later, I was visiting my mother, because Dad was in the hospital. This in itself was nothing new since he had bounced back many times during the last few years. When they let him come home, I was sure it was one of those episodes he would get over.

That night, he asked me to get him a glass of water and inquired what I was going to fix him for breakfast.

"Dad, it's 2 o'clock in the morning! I don't know what I'm going to make for you, but it will be something you like," I said as I leaned over to kiss him on the cheek. He smiled and said, "Ok."

An hour later, my mom asked me to check on him. He had died peacefully and would get his breakfast at the Lord's banqueting table in heaven. It was doubly hard for me since I had to help Mom and my family, while grieving myself for my father.

How glad I was for the experience I had gained with Comforting Friends Ministry. I had come a long way in dealing with grief since my husband and son died and was now able to face new challenges of sorrow in a much calmer way. While I still grieved over my father's death, I did not have to go through the valley of the shadow of death, but was able to trust the Lord and put my feelings, sorrows and pain into His hands. I had learned that He is able to help me sort through them when I trust in His love, understanding and compassion.

I am by no means implying that you ever get used to losing someone. What I am saying is, that the grieving process, successfully completed in your own time, will strengthen you to the point that it does not overcome or destroy you like it did before. Instead, there is a calm acceptance that brings peace in the midst of turmoil and faith in a future in spite of the terrible loss. It is like the little lamb, carried by the Shepherd on His shoulders through the raging waters of life, safe and secure and certain of His love.

"Trust in the Lord with all your heart and lean not on your own understanding. In all your ways acknowledge Him and He will direct your path." Proverbs 3:5

Chapter 21

Good Grief

𝕴s there such a thing as good grief? The shortest sentence in the Bible is "Jesus wept." There is nothing more reassuring to find out that the Lord grieved. His friend Lazarus died and "He was deeply moved in spirit and troubled". He didn't just get a little upset, He showed deep emotions and distress, not just over the death of His friends but over the unbelief of those around Him. After all, He knew He was going to resurrect him.

Just because we know our loved one is with the Lord, doesn't mean it shows lack of faith when we grieve. Actually, good grief is when you acknowledge your sorrow and then give the broken pieces of your heart to Jesus. His love is the glue that will mend it without ugly scars and chipped areas from the pain and sorrow of your loss. Hiding your grief does not make it go away.

The picture of a little girl comes to mind as she stuffs the broken vase under her bed so her mother won't find out, knowing full well there is no way it can ever be fixed, but it will lay there and collect dust in secret. If she takes it to mom instead and shows her what happened, her mother will put the pieces back together with glue and reassurance, everything will be ok. While the vase will never look as good as it once did, the little girl is comforted that it is still there in spite of the break.

This story shows we can try to put our life or that of others back together, but only God can erase the scars, chips and dents the tragedy caused. Faith and trust in Him makes for the perfect glue and is designed to restore us to complete wholeness after the loss of a loved one. God will not give up because *you* want to, but He is interested in restoring and preparing you for a future in service to those who are where you have been. Many times, His purpose for you is greater after you have gone through your grief than you could have ever accomplished without it.

Seen in this light, grief is a good thing when looking at the big picture the way the Lord does. The Glory comes when you can see God wants to raise you to a higher level of giving of yourself, your experience and knowledge as you help others through the hard times.

But if being prepared for service was all God had in mind when He allowed us to go through this grieving process, it would be rather cruel. Since God is incapable of such negative behavior, there must be something else He has for us.

While the Lord rarely explains why He takes a loved one, He offers His never-ending love to help us overcome the loss. The only way we can take advantage of it is by seeking a closer intimacy with Him on a daily basis.

"Draw near to God and He will draw near to you." James 4:3

It is this renewed dependence on God, we never thought we needed before, that will bring us to a place of a close relationship with the Lord. The Bible says, God created man to have fellowship with His Creator. He wanted to 'take a walk with him every day in the Garden and talk to him'. He still does! And for that He paid the ultimate price – He gave His only Son to die for us on the cross so that we can once again spend time with Him in the same way Adam and Eve did. Which means, the initial purpose of prayer was not to ask for help, but to be in fellowship with the Creator of the universe.

How awesome to think that this wonderful God desires to spend time with you, walk with you and talk with you on a daily basis! And while doing this, He will heal your broken heart and make you whole. This is the Glory of His love that takes away not just your sin, but the grief and sorrow you have lived with for so long. In order for Him to do this, you cannot hide these feelings, but, like the little girl in the story, give them to your Father. Only He can restore your broken heart and make you like new in order to live your life and fulfill the purpose He still has for you.

God does not want you to settle for being a patchwork of scars, chips and cracks for the rest of your life, but gives you the chance to accept His healing love which erases them so you can be a whole person again. This does not mean He wants to erase your memories of the one you lost, but remember them with joy in your heart and gratitude that they were part of your life and will be again in eternity.

This is the final goal, the finish line of your journey of grief. It is an end to sorrow and at the same time a new beginning of a new race that will take you to new life after death. It is up to you to allow Him to take you there by giving Him your sorrow and pain as you talk to Him daily. Don't be afraid to tell Him about your feelings, your doubts and fears when you do. He already knows them and understands and will love you and walk with you until you reach the finish line. He wants you to know, He does not just have love for you, HE IS LOVE! And His love is unconditional, unfailing and will never leave you nor forsake you. The moment you know that and don't doubt, His Glory will cover you and open the door to a new beginning.

That is what He did for me as time went on when I decided to give my heart not just to Him, but reach out to others as well. It is not that I was so strong on my own when faced with devastating loss, but that He was there all the time as I gave Him my grief. This is another way to apply the scripture, "Give and will be given to you." The more I give up of what I want to hold on to, the more He is able to give me what I need to be made whole.

There are still many days, even today, that I feel the loss of Allen and Micah, but it is a soft, gentle longing that will always be there. It is no longer grief, but remembering both of them with love, joy and knowing they had been a wonderful part of my life.

I have learned that dying is very much a part of living. From the moment we are conceived, we are destined to die, like everything that lives. It is only with today's technology we can prolong the inevitable and it seems to give us the illusion that death somehow is something unacceptable which should never happen.

He knew us before we were born and knows exactly when our time on this earth is over. Therefore, the death of our loved one is no surprise or accident to Him. But, praise God, He understands when we grieve and helps us through our pain and sorrow until we can grasp how much He loves us and will never leave us nor forsake us, no matter how long it takes.

My season of grief ended when I accepted His will and learned to put my trust in Him as I reached out to others, willing to serve Him until He takes me home. And just like with Allen and Micah, that moment will come according to His will, not mine. Until then, I have this wonderful hope and trust that I will not only be with Him, but with them as well. Whenever that time comes, I am ready, Praise God!

"To everything there is a season, and a time for every purpose under heaven. A time to be born, and a time to die."
Ecclesiastes 3:1-2

Chapter 22

Love Comes Softly

𝕀 was sitting in my favorite lounge chair, one of the few things I brought with me from the old house. It was a part of my life, the place where I laughed with Allen when he was alive and cried after he died. Where I held my baby and sat in agony at his passing. There was no way I could part without it when I moved to the new house.

On this particular morning, I knew I had a big decision to make, one that would change my life in ways I could not even imagine. It had been fourteen years since the evangelist gave me the prophesy that I would marry a man who was acquainted with sorrow and will love me for who I was. I had long since given up on the Word and decided the woman had made a mistake. I was content to be single and had never met anyone I would like to be with. My life was good serving the Lord in the grief ministry and in my church and I was perfectly happy to live alone for the rest of my life.

One Sunday my friend Alice told me that she noticed, Joe Steedley, a deacon in my church, changed sides when collecting the offering.

"I bet he did because of you," she laughed.

I knew she must be wrong. But then, sure enough, he was serving the offering plate in the place where I sat every Sunday and gave me a big smile when he asked me if I needed change for the offering, which was the custom in our church.

Joe's wife had passed away several months ago after forty years of marriage. His family and mine had known each other for thirty-five and I knew him to be a committed Christian man. Granted, he was a little opinionated and a man of strong convictions, which he voiced whether you asked him or not. I remember asking his wife one time,

"How can you live with this guy? He thinks he knows it all and I don't know if I could deal with that."

She laughed in her usual friendly way and followed her husband out the door. I stood, watching them leave and wondered how I would handle a marriage like that. For a moment memories of Allen flooded my mind and they brought a little smile to my face.

A few weeks later, I attended a home going service for one of our members and Joe was there. He invited me out to lunch together with a few of my other friends. But mysteriously, everyone had something else to do and that just left the two of us. I found out much later he arranged it that way so the two of us could spend some time together. He took me to a very nice place and we spent hours telling each other what was going on in our lives. It lasted into the evening.

I knew his wife had passed away and I figured he was lonely. So I invited him to come and participate in the meetings at the Comforting Friends Ministry. When he showed up, I was not surprised when he shared he was doing good and trusted the Lord.

"God never makes mistakes and I am taking my life one day at a time," he said with confidence. "My son Eleazar and his family have moved back in with me and they are adjusting quite well."

Somehow I expected nothing less from Joe, he was just that kind of a confident, strong guy. He attended a few more classes and then told me he didn't think he needed to come back.

"That's alright, we do not force anyone to come, but prefer willing participants," I told him. I was a little disappointed, but then again, since both of us were involved in several ministries at the church, we would surely run into each other. And so we did maybe three or four times a week and stopped for a small chat. We even went out to dinner a few times; and while we had a good time of fellowship, nothing serious developed, at least not on my part.

I was at work that day when my name was announced over the PA system.

"Will Ethel Perkins please come downstairs to the first floor. There is a package for you."

This was nothing new since I was the manager at the Periodontal department and received packages all the time, but they would usually bring them to the department. What was even more unusual, this was a gorgeous bouquet of flowers with a card attached that said, 'From a secret admirer". Everyone wanted to know if it was my birthday. Needless to say, the questions didn't let up all day since they couldn't quite believe I didn't know who sent them. The problem was I couldn't come up with anyone, but I was determined to find out by calling the florist.

"We cannot give you the information, ma'am because of privacy laws. What I can tell you is he was a nice gentleman," the lady said.

This totally intrigued me and I was wondering how this man knew me or what did he look like and what did he do for a living that he could afford flowers like that. I even considered co-workers, students or patients, but to no avail. At least he did not seem to be a crazy stalker or something like that.

My friend Alice was sure it was Joe, but I brushed it aside.

"There is no way, we are just friends," I said, laughing.

The flowers arrived every week for a month with the same words on the card.

Finally, one Sunday Joe walked up to me and said with a big grin,

"I am your secret admirer."

It seems, Alice got the last laugh.

That Sunday we went out to dinner. I was in a state of shock. In my wildest dreams I had not thought Joe was the one, especially since his wife had died so recently. Over the nice meal we talked things over and I agreed that we would just date by going to dinner and attend church outings together. All this was so sudden and I felt a little uneasy at first. Allen and Micah came into my mind. What would they think? But it had been sixteen years and so I decided it would be alright and might even be fun. I hadn't dated anyone in all that time.

Joe turned out to be a gentleman in every way and I began to enjoy our relationship. When I realized he was getting serious about me, I had no idea what to do. When Mom came to visit me for her birthday, I planned to take her to New York City to see the Broadway play 'The Lion King', I asked Joe if he would drive us up there. He had family in Long Island and could drop us off in Manhattan at our hotel on Friday and pick us up on Sunday.

This way Mom could check him out and help me with my decision whether to continue seeing him. I knew she had known him for years, but people do change and she was a good judge of character. I was sure he would agree right away, but it took him a month to give me an answer.

When he came to pick us up, I tried to have Mom sit up front, but she wouldn't hear of it and took her seat in the back. On the way to New York City I talked and laughed, glad to have my mom with me, when all of a sudden, Joe reached for my hand and held it. This was something new and it alarmed me a little, but I did not withdraw it. I have no idea if Mom noticed, she didn't say anything. When we got to our hotel, Joe gave me a kiss on the cheek and went on to Long Island to stay with his God-family.

Mom and I had a wonderful time. We talked and laughed and enjoyed the show. I noticed she would bring up Joe frequently, asking me what I thought of him.

"Mom, I like him fine, but we are like brother and sister, that's all."

"I have a feeling Joe thinks much more of you than just a sister, child," she said with a knowing smile.

The ride back to Philadelphia was upbeat and happy. Joe told us about his family and told me they wanted to meet me.

I was sitting in my favorite chair, confused and unsure of what to do. If I didn't want this to go any further, I would have to break up with him.

"This is moving a little fast. What do You want me to do, Lord?" I prayed out loud. "I don't know if this is what I want." And then the prophesy came into my mind. Could he be the one after all this time? He fit the description having lost his wife and he seemed to love me. "I don't want to miss what you have for me, Lord, but I need to know for sure."

I decided to keep dating him. Soon he picked me up for church events and then on Sunday morning. He treated me like a lady and it was wonderful. Pretty soon we started going out to dinner and attended events outside the church. Many times he called me at work just to say 'hello'. When he went on a month vacation travelling to Florida and Washington DC visiting family and friends, he still took time to call me and send postcards and letters. I was impressed with him staying in touch with me by telling me what he was doing and mentioning he still wanted me to meet his family when he got back.

One letter touched my heart when he told me he could not get me out of his head and did not understand since he was not looking for another wife. Since I was not looking for a husband, could this just be a cordial relationship for us? It looked like he had the same questions I did. I decided only time would tell and so we continued dating and enjoyed each other's company.

Joe was a very strong believer in his walk with the Lord and everything to him was either black or white with no room for grey or compromise. This led to some heated discussions in our relationship, since I am a strong woman with firm opinions of my own. His strong opinions bothered me and I remembered when I asked his wife how she handled them.

I had started to like him more than I wanted, but worried that we may not be on the same page on so many issues. Could a marriage with Joe work? But then I knew we both loved Jesus and it gave me hope that we might have a chance together. That, after all is the most important thing in a marriage, that we both love the Lord and serve Him.

Two things Joe was adamant about he could never do as a Christian. One was going to movies and the other listening to secular music. The problem was, I was just as strong in believing that movies are no different from TV, what you don't like you don't watch or listen to. Talking about our differences one day, Joe agreed to go and watch 'The Passion of the Christ" with me. It softened his attitude considerably and when I told him about a secular song I had bought, he agreed to listen to it when he came over for dinner one day. It became "our" song and is called 'You make Me feel Brand-New.

As time went on, I still thought Joe was opinionated and acted like he knew it all. He prided himself that no one could beat him in quoting scripture or telling you about the Lord. It worried me a little, but if this was the man the Lord had for me, I knew our relationship would work out.

When Joe returned from another trip to Long Island, he confided in me that he had talked to his godmother about me. She told him,

"If you love this young lady, pray and ask what the Lord is saying you are to do."

When he asked the Lord, He got a clear message,

"You are her Boaz and she is your Ruth. You are to be her redeemer."

"There is surely a future hope for you, and your hope will not be cut off." Proverbs 23:18

Chapter 23

You make me feel brand-new

$\mathfrak{I}$ was shaken to the core. Was this really the man the Lord had for me? I was not sure about my feelings, but had no idea what it was that held me back. Was it Allen? Or maybe Micah? I didn't know what to think. So many years had passed without them, I was no longer able to feel clearly what they might want me to do. I had been alone for all this time and felt confused. I was sixty-one years old, too old to get used to another man. Allen and Micah were my family, my heroes and the two men I loved beyond anything. There were no doubts, no fear or uncertainty in my relationship with them. What about Joe, could I ever love him like that?

"I am not sure about my feelings for you, Joe,' I told him that day. If you still want to date me on that basis, I am willing to go out with you until I know for certain."

"I am fine with that, because I don't want to lose you," he said. "You are worth waiting for."

Several weeks went by. One day, Joe turned up at work and asked me to go to lunch with him.

"I'm really not dressed up enough to go to lunch in Center City Philadelphia," I said, after he told me where we were going. "If I had known I would have put on a better set of nursing scrubs," I added, a little put out.

"You look great, just let me take you to a special place," he said as he took my arm.

I was expecting a restaurant, but instead he led me to the jewelry district in the city. I was confused as I looked around the store at the expensive merchandise laid out in glass showcases.

"Feel free to look at anything you want, I will get it out for you," the owner said. After hesitating a second, I realized, Joe brought me here to pick out an engagement ring. Like a kid in a candy story, I didn't know where to begin and wondered around as if in a daze, looking at the glittering diamond rings everywhere. Suddenly, there was one that caught my eye. It was big and bold and I liked it. Before I pointed to it, I stopped and made myself point at a much smaller one, because I didn't want Joe to get into financial trouble.

"Are you sure that is the one you want?" Joe asked.

"Well, there is another one, but it is too expensive," I said, and pointed at the big one.

Joe and the jeweler looked at each other and laughed.

"That's the one I had picked out for you," he said and handed it to me. I was overwhelmed as I tried it on.

"You two seem to have the same taste," the man said. "Many engagements have broken up in this store, because couples cannot agree on the rings." He was beaming, "I think you two are going to have a good future together."

I was happy.

There was no lunch that day. It was very hard for me not to tell everyone, because we had to leave the ring to have it sized for me. It would not be ready until next Friday. It felt like waiting for Christmas. A whole week!

The Friday finally came. I had invited Joe for dinner. It was the first time he was at my house alone. I was hoping he would be romantic when he gave me the ring. And he was! It was after we finished dinner, he took out the ring, got down on his knees and said, Lee Ethel Perkins, would you do me the honor of becoming my wife?"

"I looked at him, my eyes filled with happiness and love and said, "Yes." All the doubt was gone and I thanked God that He had fulfilled His promise of giving me a husband who would love me for myself. How faithful our Lord is! It took fourteen years for His Word to be fulfilled and He had never left me or forsaken me during my treacherous journey through grief and sorrow. Joe and I asked Him to lead and guide us in the way we should go in our future together.

The following Saturday we had an appointment with our pastor Bishop Morris and told him of our engagement. Since I was the announcer in the service, I could not very well do it. The next Sunday at the end of the service, the pastor asked for a drum roll and asked for Joe and me to come up front to the cheers of the congregation. They came running up front to congratulate us and treated us like royalty. It was a joyous occasion with good wishes and many blessings.

It was several days later, Joe asked me if I had read the inscription on the ring.

"I had no idea there was one," I said as I took it off my finger. And there it was: Two become one. JLS-LE

God's faithfulness is astounding. When He gives us a Word, it may take a while to be fulfilled, but He never forgets to bring it to pass. In the midst of the storm He has our life in His hand and knows how to bring us through stronger and better than we were before.

I still mourn the death of my two loved ones and wish they could be with me, but I also know we are all in His perfect will. While I still have a purpose to accomplish here on earth, theirs is a life with Him in eternity. I am very sure they have an even bigger work than mine since they are in the presence of the Lord. While I have no idea what that might be, I am absolutely certain their life is one of a higher calling in the center of God's will. I am content and know I will see them again.

When grief comes to an end, it leads to a new beginning. The wonderful memories will always be with me as I get ready to embark on a new marriage, a new place to live and a new life. The only thing that remains a constant is God's love and mercy. I know today, He is a God whose Word is truth. I have experienced to the fullest that I can trust Him with my life and my future.

"The Lord is my light and my salvation – whom shall I fear? The Lord is the stronghold of my life – of who shall I be afraid?"
Psalm 27:1

"I will exalt you, O Lord, for you lifted me up out of the depth and did not let my enemies gloat over me.
O Lord my God, I called to you for help and you healed me.
O Lord, you brought me up from the grave, you spared me from going down into the pit.
Sing to the Lord, you saints of his, praise His holy name."
Psalm 30:1-4

Chapter 24

And the Two shall become One

While I had said 'yes' when Joe asked me to marry him, I still had many doubts whether this is what the Lord wanted me to do. I had been single for sixteen years and had gotten used to doing things my way. He was a strong, opinionated man with strict views on matters concerning all things, but especially his faith and the do's and don'ts about how to live it. I viewed myself as more flexible and less black and white and I was scared we would not find common ground in important matters in daily living and spiritual beliefs.

As the day of our wedding drew closer, I was getting extremely nervous and pleaded with the Lord to give me a sign whether to go through with it.

"Show me what to do, Lord and I will obey you," I prayed that day during my prayer time. "I need to know." I opened up my devotional book and it fell open to the Song of Solomon in the fifth chapter in the first few verses. It is the story about the young woman whose lover came knocking on her door but she would not let him in. When she finally did open it, he was gone and no matter how she looked for him, she could not find him and her heart was broken.

I was deeply touched as I read the account and realized the Lord was telling me not to turn Joe away, but to accept him as my Boaz with me being his Ruth. I cried as I gave God thanks and praise for telling me what to do and take Joe as my husband. I finally felt at peace about it and began to feel joy at the prospect of my upcoming marriage. The Lord had answered my plea and I suddenly knew the prophesy had come to pass that I would marry a man who truly loved me.

Both of our families were happy. They had been friends for many years and this bound us even closer together. Everyone wanted to help and be a part of the preparations. What a happy time! We were now being invited everywhere as a couple and it made me feel good. So I was not surprised when one of my friends, Odessa and her husband asked us for dinner for my birthday. What I didn't know, it was to be a surprise engagement celebration as well.

The next Saturday, my friend Joyce and I were supposed to meet at the home of our consultant of Comforting Friends Dr. Joe Crumbley, who is a psychologist and the husband of my good friend Carol. When we got to their home, we could barely find a place to park. Because of a yard sale next door, I didn't wonder about the many cars and even stopped to look around for a moment. To my surprise it turned out to be a bridal shower with ladies from church, co-workers, some of my family and neighbors from the old neighborhood.

The wedding day was fast approaching and there were so many things to do. Margaret, the seamstress of the church had made me a beautiful, floor length three-piece suit in soft pink with a matching vest for Joe. Winnifred made my bridal bouquet in the same soft pink and it was beautiful.

The wedding party was very simple with my sister Jean as maid of honor and my brother John walking me down the aisle. Joes son Eleazar was his best man. The wedding ceremony had been announced in church that Sunday and would take place right before the benediction. I left the service in time to change into my wedding outfit and was surprised to find the congregation had stayed. It made me very nervous when I returned and found so many were still there. I was beginning to feel shaky, not because of fear, but I had forgotten to eat anything and was afraid I would be one of those brides who pass out at the altar!

Mrs. Ruby sang our favorite song "You Made Me Feel Brand-new." She did a great job and when she was finished she walked over to Joe and handed him the microphone. He turned toward me and sang *our* song to me. I was overwhelmed with joy as we kissed after Bishop Morris finally pronounced us man and wife. It was April 25, 2004.

The first three weeks of our marriage we spent traveling to Williamsburg in Virginia, New York City and from there on a cruise to the Caribbean. On our return we lived in Joe's house since it was a two-story and I put mine on the market. I decided to leave my favorite lounge chair behind. With a little sadness I realized it was time to part with it. It was a new life, a new beginning with a new husband.

My house did not sell until three months later and when I signed the papers I fully realized that I had begun a new life and would leave behind the old for good. The Lord had been with me during those hard years and had kept me in His love each and every day.

After I retired a year later, Joe and I moved to a small town in Central Florida. But not before my work place as well as the church gave us a proper send-off. On November 2, 2005 the church gave us an Appreciation and Farewell Service, honoring us as Faithful Servants of God and Pioneer Members for almost 40 years.

We moved into new home in a retirement community build to our specifications shortly before Thanksgiving of 2005. Moving so far away from home, I decided to have a butterfly memorial tree build in the backyard so I will always be reminded of my wonderful son Micah.

The butterfly personifies for me how we start out in the grieving process from the ugly larvae to the cocoon, hiding safely in the protective arms of the Lord, only to emerge as the beautiful, changed child of God soaring into the light of restoration and freedom. Micah and Allen have made it even one step further. They have become one with the Son, transformed into glorious beings in the presence of the Lord.

Looking back over my journey I now see how God has restored to me all that I thought I had lost forever. I am no longer alone like I feared, because He gave me a wonderful husband. I am a mother again, because I have Joe's son and grandchildren to call my own. I have joy and fulfilment again as together with Joe we serve as Deacons in a great church, where I am also leading a grief ministry.

The faithfulness of my God overwhelms me as I count my blessings daily. And this is why I wanted to write my story, to share with you how you too can overcome and soar once again like an eagle on the current of faith. While Allen and Micah will always be in my heart and my love for them will never diminish, the Lord has given me a new and exciting life while I remain in His service on this earth. There are no limitations with God, His mercies and His love last forever and are new every morning. And while He does not shield us form trials and problems, He is there with us, always urging us on to trust Him to fulfill the purpose He created us for. It is this future we hold on to when we find ourselves in the midst of grief.

To be a survivor of enormous loss is to have reached the Glory of His love and emerge on the other side a new creature like the butterfly. Its brilliant colors represent the triumph and joy of living in the light of the Son of God as we soar toward an even more shining eternity, never to experience sorrow and grief again.

Are you ready to face this wonderful future by giving your life to the Lord Jesus Christ? If you have not done so, please pray this prayer with me so that you can come out of your pain and into the Light of a God who loves you enough that He sent His only Son to die on the cross for you.

Dear Father in Heaven,

I am weary and filled with sorrow and grief. I cannot handle my life on my own any longer. I feel broken and alone and I miss my loved one. Please accept me into your protective arms as I surrender my life to You. I believe that You are my God and sent your Son Jesus to die for me, that He rose from the dead and will come again. I want to be Your child and trust You to help me with my grief and give me a future and a hope to become that butterfly You want me to be. I ask this in Jesus Name.

The End

I ask the Lord to bless you and hope that my story has helped you with your grief. If you have someone who has lost a loved one, tell them about this book and encourage them to find a grief support group.

Also, please be so kind to help others who are grieving by writing a review on Amazon. Even if you have not bought it through Amazon, you can still go there to share how much it has helped you. It is a wonderful way to share how God can be trusted and will be there for all who ask Him and so find a way to overcome and be victorious. And that includes YOU!

This book is available on Amazon.com in paperback and on Kindle.

Made in the USA
Columbia, SC
14 February 2019